BUFFALO, BARRELS, & BOURBON

Other Books by F. Paul Pacult

Kindred Spirits: The Spirit Journal Guide to the World's Distilled Spirits and Fortified Wines (Hyperion, 1997)

The Beer Essentials: The Spirit Journal Guide to Over 650 of the World's Beers (Hyperion, 1997)

American Still Life: The Jim Beam Story and the Making of the World's #1 Bourbon (John Wiley & Sons, 2003)

A Double Scotch: How Chivas Regal and The Glenlivet Became Global Icons (John Wiley & Sons, 2005)

Kindred Spirits 2: 2,400 Reviews of Whiskey, Brandy, Vodka, Tequila, Rum, Gin, and Liqueurs from F. Paul Pacult's Spirit Journal 2000–2007 (Spirit Journal, Inc., 2008)

The New Kindred Spirits: More Than 2,000 All-New Reviews of Whiskey, Brandy, Gins, Vodkas, Agave Spirits, Rum, Amari, Bitters, and Liqueur from F. Paul Pacult's Spirit Journal (Matt Holt Books, 2021)

F. PAUL PACULT

BUFFALO, BARRELS, & BOURBON

THE STORY OF HOW BUFFALO TRACE DISTILLERY BECAME THE WORLD'S MOST AWARDED DISTILLERY

WILEY

Published by John Wiley & Sons, Inc., Hoboken, New Jersey.
Published simultaneously in Canada.

For general information on our other products and services or for technical support, please contact our Customer Care Department within the United States at (800) 762-2974, outside the United States at (317) 572-3993 or fax (317) 572-4002.

Wiley also publishes its books in a variety of electronic formats. Some content that appears in print may not be available in electronic formats. For more information about Wiley products, visit our web site at www.wiley.com.

Library of Congress Cataloging-in-Publication Data is Available:

ISBN: 9781394321650 (paperback)
ISBN: 9781119599920 (ePub)
ISBN: 9781119599937 (ePDF)

Cover Design: Wiley
Cover Images: © Buffalo Trace Distillery
Author Photo: © Michael Gold/The Corporate Image

SKY10094343_121924

For Sue

Contents

Acknowledgments

I HAVE A WHOLE scorecard of generous people to thank for their assistance with the writing of this book. First of all, Matt Holt, the former Wiley publisher who approached Sue and me about writing a third book for Wiley, along with our present-day Wiley publisher Shannon Vargo. I appreciate their staunch support of *Buffalo, Barrels, & Bourbon*. Senior Editor Sally Baker and Managing Editor Deborah Schindlar at Wiley have been veritable rocks and a delight to deal with. Kudos also go to my friend Sarah Tirone for poring over the manuscript at a critical stage of development and telling, with candor, what she thought of it. Whiskey journalist/blogger/author Chuck Cowdery freely offered his keen insights along the way, both in person and via his many unvarnished blog postings. Thank you, Chuck. My appreciation also goes to colleague and celebrated whiskey writer Liza Weisstuch for her insightful viewpoints. Both the Filson Historical Society and the Kentucky Historical Society deserve a tip of my hat for their very existence, as well as the assistance their archives provided throughout the book's research period. Never standing in the way of where my independent research was leading me, the management and public relations teams at Buffalo Trace deserve shout-outs for their no-strings-attached cooperation, fully cognizant that my findings might in the end differ with their own data. A special note of appreciation goes to Buffalo Trace archivist Madison Sevilla, whose patience and diligence were pivotal in pointing out directions for deeper research. I would be remiss if I didn't note and acknowledge American whiskey historian Carolyn Brooks for sharing her superb investigative paper, "A Leestown Chronology," which cleared many obstacles and bridged gaps on my fact-finding path. Last, but certainly not least, thanks to my wife, collaborator, master editor, and partner Sue Woodley for, well, everything.

Introduction

MY PROFESSION IS COMMUNING with spirits. Since 1989, I have formally reviewed over 30,000 of the fermented and distilled consumable liquids commonly referred to as "spirits," "distillates," "water of life," or, more scurrilously, "firewater," "hooch," "booze," "sauce," or "hard liquor." In addition to my subscription-only newsletter *F. Paul Pacult's Spirit Journal*, these product evaluations, sometimes with accompanying feature stories, have appeared in scores of publications over the past three decades. These included the *New York Times* Sunday magazine, *Wine Enthusiast*, *Playboy*, *Delta Sky* in-flight magazine, *Wine & Spirits*, *Men's Journal*, *Beverage Dynamics*, *Cheers*, and many more. Wearing another of my career hats, for two decades I have consulted to numerous beverage companies, assisting them either in the creation of new spirit brands or helping them to revitalize old ones. In one such instance, I have turned master blender for an American whiskey portfolio, Jacob's Pardon. Then there is my spirits education hat, but on this I'll spare you details, saving them for the next time.

After plying my trade in this manner for over 30 years, I have come to many conclusions. Perhaps the most salient determination I have made is this: of all the spirits that illuminate the galaxy of distilled potables, whiskey is my hands-down favorite. As charming as it can be, whiskey is a perplexing spirits category, one that is on occasion disconcerting and, at its most extreme, impenetrable. Yet for all its manifold complexities, every whiskey is composed of only three easily obtained, foundational ingredients: grain, water, and yeast. After being fermented and distilled, freshly made whiskeys are placed in cocoon-like barrels wherein they undergo periods of complicated metamorphosis. Once released from captivity in the aging warehouses, the world's whiskeys take the international stage as the most prized and expensive of all distillates. They are the monarch butterflies of the spirits category. They can be, and frequently are, great hooch, in other words.

One of whiskey's most enduring mysteries is why one can be so wildly dissimilar in character traits from another, not just from nation to nation or region to region, but even from barrel to barrel of the same batch. If all of the world's whiskeys are made from but a trio of commonplace, wholly familiar ingredients, how can they differ so markedly in personality? Moreover, why are a handful of the whiskey distillers more adept at the art of whiskey making than others? What are their secrets? I've been asking these questions for over three decades.

Three years ago, John Wiley & Sons, Inc., the Hoboken, New Jersey–based publisher of two previous books of mine, *American Still Life* (2003) and *A Double Scotch* (2005), contacted me, expressing an interest in backing another spirits-oriented business book. The topic choice, they said, was up to me. After some weeks of consideration deciding between proposing another book on Scotch whisky or one more on American whiskey, I settled on a subject that had all the earmarks of timeliness and pertinence: the meteoric rise in prominence of the Buffalo Trace Distillery in Frankfort, Kentucky. Along with a chapter and verse accounting of this distillery's emergence since before the nineteenth century, my other hope was to perhaps answer at least some of my queries about a few of whiskey's inherent riddles.

Wiley agreed to my proposal and the deal was struck. Upon informing the distillery operators about the project, I made arrangements to meet with their archivists to peruse their voluminous records. The top executives at Buffalo Trace at the time, namely CEO Mark Brown, public relations manager Amy Preske, master distiller Harlen Wheatley, master blender Drew Mayville, and former senior marketing director Kris Comstock (who departed early in 2021), have all known me long enough to know that I would allow the facts of the historical records as I unearthed them to dictate the trajectory of the story, warts and all. As with *American Still Life* and *A Double Scotch*, my independence would not permit a vanity project. They acknowledged that my views might in the end differ with theirs and to their credit offered me their assistance, encouragement, and direct access to the company archives. Nothing more.

As an active spirits critic, I have grown intimately familiar with the bourbon and rye whiskeys produced in abundance at their historic plant, which is now a celebrated landmark. As the research data unfolded over many months of examination, I became convinced that Buffalo Trace's history deserved to be told as much from the viewpoint of its low-bank location on the Kentucky River as from the intriguing lives of the people who created the legendary bourbon and rye whiskeys through the decades. The striking history of the distillery's site was, in my view, of paramount importance to the proper telling of the story. The tale of Buffalo Trace Distillery, I concluded early on, could not have occurred at any other place.

Consequently, reading after looking through the Glossary, which I suggest, you will find that the initial chapters have little to do with the bubbling of fermenting grain mash or the boiling of the mash's low-strength beer into high-alcohol distillate. The opening pages of *Buffalo, Barrels, & Bourbon*, nearly a fifth of the narrative, instead deals with the stark realities endured by the robust seventeenth-, eighteenth-, and early nineteenth-century Euro-American individuals who survived and persevered in the harsh, but green and lush North American environment. In this case, the focus lies on the uncharted, heavily forested area described first in maps as *Kentucke*. While beguiling to the eye and imagination, the deceptively feral soul of Kentucke forced hundreds of the earliest explorers, surveyors, military scouts, trappers, and fur traders to their knees in bruised submission. At least, it did for those fortunate ones who lived long enough to talk or write about it in journals.

The land itself where the Buffalo Trace Distillery campus stands today is a listed member of the National Register of Historic Places (#2428), one of a mere 2,600 such sites in the United States. This location in north-central Kentucky is the beneficiary of a geological and topographical majesty that must have been breathtaking to the first Euro-Americans who hacked their way through the midnight-dark primeval forests and paddled their pirogues down the swirling currents of the Kentucky River. It is here where the layers of sedentary substrata, the karst shelf geology, the trough-like sandy bank, pure spring water, the fertile, arable land for the growing of corn, and the strategic proximity to a major waterway, the Ohio River, all merge to create an ideal situation in which to make whiskey. Over time, the spilt blood of the pioneers, the heinous trials endured by the Native American tribes, and the near extinction of the dominant beast of the Great Plains, the buffalo, converged to create this saga about the taming of this virgin region and, later, about the distilling of legendary American whiskey.

After the low-bank location was settled with the building of crude riverside log structures, the storyline changes into a narrative that centers upon the multiple generations of influential clans, such as the Lees, Swigerts, Taylors, Staggs, Blantons, and Van Winkles. Painted with the main characters' foibles, peccadilloes, aspirations, failures, ingenuity, courage, and triumphs, *Buffalo, Barrels, & Bourbon* then warps into the chapters that uncover the evolution of some of America's most beloved whiskeys, the bourbons and ryes of Buffalo Trace.

The research and writing of this book took me back to places in time and space that I'd not visited to any significant degree for some years. It was grand to be immersed once again in the racehorse and whiskey fables of Kentucky's Bluegrass district. If bourbon whiskey is, as many believe, America's hallmark spirit, Kentucky is its cradle, its ancestral place of origin, its soul and vibrant inspiration.

F. PAUL PACULT
Hudson Valley, New York
Spring 2021

Glossary

It would be unfair to assume that everyone who picks up *Buffalo, Barrels, & Bourbon* will be sufficiently versed in the often arcane terminology related to whiskey and its production. Therefore, in the interest of leveling the linguistic playing field from the beginning, I am including this brief glossary upfront to assist in making better sense of some commonly utilized words in the American whiskey lexicon. Think of this as being your first sip.

Alcohol by volume   Also known globally as "abv"; the international measure of how many milliliters (mL) of pure ethanol exist in 100 mL of a liquid at precisely 20 degrees Centigrade (68 degrees Fahrenheit). It's the ratio between alcohol and water. By the liter, then, a bottle that is identified as 43 percent alcohol also has 57 percent water. All American whiskeys are at least 40 percent alcohol by volume as decreed by statute.

Barrel proof   Whiskey that is bottled directly from the barrel and released at the full alcohol by volume strength, undiluted, meeting the truth-in-labeling requirements laid down by the U.S. Bureau of Alcohol, Tobacco and Firearms, ruling 79-9.

Blended whiskey   Legal whiskeys that by American law are composed of a minimum of 20 percent straight whiskey and other spirits, most typically neutral grain spirits (NGS), in order to create a low-cost, high-volume whiskey.

Bottled-in-bond   In accordance with the Bottled-in-Bond Act of 1897, an American whiskey or spirit that comes from one distillation season (January–June or July–December), is then matured for at least four years in a federally bonded and supervised warehouse, and is bottled at 50 percent alcohol by volume. Most bottled-in-bond spirits are whiskey.

Bourbon whiskey By law (Federal Standards of Identity for Distilled Spirits, code 27 CFR §5.22(b)(1)(i)) must be made within the United States; must be at a minimum 51 percent corn; must be aged in new, charred oak containers; must be distilled not higher than 80 percent alcohol; must go into the aging barrel at no higher than 62.5 percent alcohol by volume; and must be bottled at no lower than 40 percent abv. Bourbon labeled as *Straight Bourbon* must, by law, be matured in new, charred oak containers for at least two years and cannot have anything added to it, such as coloring or flavoring.

Char level One of the key requirements for straight whiskeys made in the United States is that they be matured in new, charred oak barrels (containers) for at least two years. Charring briefly over roaring flames of fire accomplishes several things, including altering some of the wood's chemical compounds, which prepares them for more advantageous contact with the virgin whiskey. Four levels of charring are traditionally employed, with level one being the lightest and level four being the deepest and most impactful. Experiments using even more severely charred barrels are ongoing. (I could discuss this topic at length for days, but not here.)

Light whiskey Defined in January 1968 by U.S. government regulation, these whiskeys must be distilled to between 80 and 95 percent alcohol by volume and can be matured in either previously used or uncharred new barrels for any length of time.

Mash bill Basically this is the recipe for the ratios of grains used in American whiskey; for example, straight bourbons are always created from mash bills that are made up of at least 51 percent corn with supplemental grains such as rye and malted barley or wheat and malted barley. Straight rye whiskeys mash bills must contain a minimum of 51 percent rye. Mash bills vary from distiller to distiller, depending entirely on the style of whiskey they prefer.

Proof The variant measure of ethanol content in a beverage from alcohol by volume, whose origin arose in sixteenth-century England for taxation purposes. In the United States, proof is calculated as being twice the measure of abv, so 50 percent abv whiskey is 100 proof.

Rickhouse/Rackhouse A traditional aging warehouse located within the United States, one that houses barreled whiskey for maturation in ascending wooden or metal racks, known as "ricks," or on wooden pallets. Barrels are mostly laid horizontally, though some strategies have them vertically aligned (in palletized warehouses). Up to 20,000 barrels can be stored in a typical rickhouse. A federally bonded rickhouse is supervised by government agents. Free warehouses are not controlled by government agents. Rickhouses come in different construction variations, such as masonry with frames of concrete or steel, palletized, one-story flathouses, and steel-clad, with corrugated steel facings.

Rye whiskey As a straight whiskey, rye must adhere to the regulations that dictate all American straight whiskeys. Must be at least 51 percent rye grain, must be aged in new, charred oak containers for a minimum of two years, must not be distilled to higher than 80 percent abv, and must not be barreled at more than 62.5 percent.

Sour mash Mash is a mixture of grain, water, and malt, used in the creation of sourdough bread (the starter) and a majority of American whiskeys. Sour mash is a production process in which a portion of a previous mash is held back and then added to the next mash to trigger fermentation. This is done to improve overall quality and consistency of whiskey by exerting greater control over the growth of unwanted yeasts and bacteria, which could have adverse effects on the final product.

Straight whiskey Must be produced from a minimum of 51 percent, respectively, of corn, rye, wheat, malted barley or malted rye; cannot be distilled to higher than 80 percent abv; cannot be entered into a barrel at higher than 62.5 percent abv; the containers must be charred, new oak containers aged for at least two years. These include straight bourbon, straight rye.

Whiskey/whisky The spelling of *whiskey* with and without the *e* is a confounding side issue. Distillers in Scotland, India, Japan, and Canada prefer *whisky* while those in Ireland and most distillers in the United States utilize *whiskey*. To make it even more confusing, a handful of American distillers, namely Makers Mark, George Dickel, and Old Forester use *whisky*. Why should this be straightforward?

And so, we begin . . .

I

"This River Runes North West and Out of ye Westerly Side . . ."

THE EXACT SPOT on which the story of Buffalo Trace Distillery begins is in the northern reaches of the Commonwealth of Kentucky, known as Bluegrass, the verdant region immediately south of the state of Ohio. This location, whose precise coordinates are 38.2167°N, 84.8709°W, is ordinary by most mid-continental topographical standards. It is just a low, dipping bank, a sandy crossing point along the serpentine Kentucky River. However, since the late twentieth century, this site has become a hallowed destination for whiskey lovers, specifically because of the present-day distillery, its engrossing history, and its acclaimed roster of award-winning rye and bourbon whiskeys.

To best set the stage with regard to this point on the North American map and its recent occupant, it is necessary to first time-travel back 11,500 to 12,000 years to the cold, bleak conclusion of planet Earth's Pleistocene

Epoch. This frigid period was the bracing remnant, an echo of the Northern Hemisphere's last great Ice Age. North America's two towering, blue-tinted glaciers, the Laurentide that lay east of the Mississippi River and the Cordilleran that lay to the river's west, were slowly receding northward into Canada. In their wake, the glaciers, at some points two miles thick, left great swaths of hardwood forests, carved river valleys and fathomless glacial lakes, grassy pastures, and vast, desolate, and arid plains.

Archaeologists postulate that as long ago as 9500–8000 BCE (Before Common Era) the hunter-gatherer ancestors of today's Native Americans were already active in the area of North America that encompasses parts of the present-day states of Illinois, Indiana, Ohio, Tennessee, Missouri, West Virginia, New York, Virginia, and Kentucky. Geologists refer to this distinctive area as the Salina Basin, a sprawling region south of the Great Lakes that is rich in deep layers of minerals and rock-salt deposits.[1] Tribal histories point out that the Native Americans utilized salt as a condiment. In the slowly warming environmental conditions of the period, the small, nomadic groups of indigenous hunters became skilled in stalking big game, including mammalian behemoths like the wooly mammoth, bison, short-faced bear, dire wolf, ground sloth, and mastodon. Other predators included smilodons, the huge and ferocious genus of saber-toothed cats that without fuss or hesitation efficiently preyed on all mammals, including the era's scrawny, but swift and clever *homo sapiens* (Latin, "wise man").

During the same period, a fateful North American event, called the "Pleistocene megafauna extinction," occurred. In the relatively brief span of hundreds of years, as many as 90 genera of megafauna, that group of large mammals weighing more than 100 pounds, vanished due to a docket of still-speculative reasons. These possible causes included the gyrations in global climate as the Earth incrementally warmed; evolving terrain due to volcanic or seismic activity; widespread drought; overhunting by the increasingly adept and resourceful aboriginal tribes; and, perhaps most spectacularly, the yet-to-be discovered impact of an asteroid. Though major annihilations of plant, insect, and animal life have regularly occurred throughout the annuls of the Earth's history, no overwhelming body of evidence points to a single cause of such an extreme destruction of large mammals as the Pleistocene era closed. Most likely, this mass elimination happened due to a confluence of two or more of the cited causes. One result of significant note, however, involves one member of Pleistocene megafauna that somehow survived this cataclysmic event: the rugged bison.

With the heating up of North America's climate through the Archaic Period of 8000–1000 BCE, conditions in the Salina Basin region became more tolerable for the growing numbers of native peoples who populated the Bluegrass. Critically, fresh water was plentiful in the area presently known as Kentucky, as were big game and fresh water fish. The northwesterly flowing Kentucky and Licking rivers and their tributaries, along with cold-water springs, sinkholes, lakes and ponds formed through crevices in the karst, or limestone ridge, known as the Cincinnati Arch, created an accommodating habitat in which flora, fauna, and the hunter-gatherer native peoples could survive.

In the 2,000-year period that is known as the "Woodland Period," from 1000 BCE to 1000 CE (Common Era), the social structure of the tribal populace grew more complex, as more permanent communities and residential compounds, some based upon primitive agriculture, began to be established. Pottery and basket-weaving became important skills and cultural emblems that defined tribal identities. The cultivation of crops centered mostly on the "three sisters" of Pan-American agriculture, beans, squash, and maize (also known as Indian corn), but also included the seasonal growing of amaranth, sunflower, and tobacco. By 450 BCE, the tribes started to build burial mounds in northern Kentucky, signaling another characteristic of a community-oriented society and the conclusion, at least in part, of nomadic lifestyles. The intersecting river system of the Bluegrass provided convenient highways by bark canoe or dugout that promoted inter-tribal trade and the movement between the Shawnee, Cherokee, Chickasaw, Wyandot, Delaware, Mosopelea, and Yuchi hunting camps.

Once the Americas were pried open by the voyages of Christopher Columbus in the 1490s, European monarchs rushed to gain footholds in the exotic continents to the west for the express purposes of mining their untapped natural resources, in particular, gold, silver, and beaver furs, and to claim territory for the expansion of their kingdoms. Spain and Portugal were especially active in exploration throughout the sixteenth century. Their aggressive exploits caused deep concern in the courts of their main commercial and military rivals, England and France.

Then, in 1607, a century prior to the formation of the Kingdom of Great Britain, three vessels sailing under the flag of England landed at what is now coastal Virginia. They were members of the chartered Virginia Company. Their mission was to create a colony, to be christened Jamestown, in North America for the English monarch King James I. Jamestown's harrowing struggles with famine, disease, and bitter clashes with the Algonquin tribe are widely known.

In 1609, James I proclaimed the vast expanse of lands northwest and west of Virginia, that included the area that would later become Kentucky, as the property of the royal colony. With that event as well as earlier incursions by the French and Spanish, the days of the eastern native tribes' reign became numbered. In the latter half of the seventeenth century, initial forays from Spanish and French Jesuit priests, trappers, and explorers like Robert de la Salle, Jacques Marquette, and Louis Jolliet deep into the North American heartland had already taken place. From 1650 to 1675, expeditions led by Euro-American colonists from Virginia and North Carolina traveling as far west as the Mississippi River passed through northern Kentucky, provoking the native tribes.

A remarkably vivid letter written on August 22, 1674 at Fort Henry in colonial Virginia by fur trader Colonel Abraham Wood to London-based investor John Richards described in startling detail the expeditions of two explorers, James Needham and Gabriel Arthur, Wood's servant.[2] Ten jam-packed pages of derring-do chronicle their exploits over the course of two years, depicting with aching clarity the severity of the trials posed by such ventures of the period. Colonel Wood in April 1673 commissioned Needham and Arthur to venture into the wild regions west of the Virginia and Carolina colonies in order to reach a trade agreement with the Cherokee tribe. The letter addresses how the men ". . . killd many swine, sturgin [sturgeon] and beavers and barbecued them . . ." It spoke of Needham and Arthur's numerous tense encounters with the suspicious native tribes. In one intriguing passage, Wood speaks of how "This river runes north west

and out of ye westerly side it goeth another great river about a days journey lower where the inhabitance are an inumarable company of Indians
. . ." It is clear from the report that Needham and Arthur's travels covered
a wide range of territory that lay directly to the west of the Virginia and
North Carolina colonies. The language suggests that their journeys might
well have included northern Kentucky, where two rivers, the Kentucky
and the Licking, run in a northwesterly direction.

James Needham unfortunately came to a horrific end at the hands of a
tribal warrior and guide called Occhonechee Indian John, ". . . a fatt thick
bluff faced fellow . . ." who reportedly first shot Needham ". . . neare ye
burr of ye eare . . ." after a heated, day-long disagreement. He then hacked
open Needham's chest with a tomahawk, ripped out his heart, and held it
aloft for all his companions to see. Wood's account of James Needham's
death reported, ". . . ye Tomahittans started to rescue Needham but Indian
John was too quick for them, soe died the heroyick English man."

Arthur barely survived the violence, ending up first as a captive but
later as a trusted companion of the tribal chief of the native band referred
to by Wood as Tomahittans, more commonly known as Cherokees. After
being wounded in the arm from an arrow, taking part in war party raids
on Spanish settlements in Florida, and marrying a Tomahittan woman
named Hannah Rebecca Nikitie, Gabriel Arthur eventually returned to
Fort Henry on June 18, 1674, after roving back and forth through what is
now Kentucky, Alabama, Georgia, Florida, and Tennessee over the course
of nearly two nerve-racking years. Abraham Wood's commercial ambitions in the frontier ceased with James Needham's demise and Gabriel
Arthur's final return.[3]

Yet even facing such horrors, exploratory penetrations into the western frontier continued unabated and were often underwritten by companies like the Ohio Company of Virginia, the Illinois and Wabash Land
Company, and the Ohio Land Company.[4] The explorers, surveyors, traders, trappers, blacksmiths, carpenters, and hunters of the pre–American
Revolutionary War period who journeyed westward over the crags of the
Blue Ridge and Appalachian mountain chains to trek into the inhos-
pitable environs of the Ohio River Valley were intrepid, rugged, and
determined individuals. A substantial number of the adventurers who

ventured into this desolate region in the seventeenth and eighteenth centuries were never seen or heard from again. Others, either broken in spirit or maimed by bear claw or arrowhead or copperhead snake, returned chastened to the safety of the 13 Atlantic coast-hugging American colonies that were by the 1760s ruled by King George III, monarch of Great Britain. Their quests and dreams, as documented by volumes of existing accounts, often ended in defeat, ill health, or financial ruin. The taverns of Philadelphia, the beer halls of Boston, and the inns of Richmond served as the theatres in which the defeated travelers recounted their bedeviled wanderings. They spun bone-chilling tales of starvation, of lost fingers and toes to frostbite, of impenetrable forests, of lethal midnight attacks by panthers or feral pigs and, most frightening of all, their gruesome encounters with hunting and war parties of native tribes. Such was the misfortune for some after being subdued by the harsh rigors of the unforgiving western wilderness.

By stark contrast, the more successful returning wayfarers from the frontier came back to the colonies in triumph, brandishing bundles of animal pelts, the scars of hair-raising escapades, and unbridled hubris. With infectious gusto, they reported to mesmerized colonial audiences about a limitless, fertile, Garden of Eden–like paradise that, yes, tested any sane person's deepest inner resources and nerve, but likewise offered to those blessed with a surfeit of mettle the potential reward of witnessing virgin, uncharted lands on which to hunt and fish and perhaps, in time, to cultivate and settle. One later report carried by the *Courier Journal of Louisville* on September 9, 1888, that focused on the escapades of one family, the McAfee clan, stated, "The glowing description given of the country beyond the mountains, by Dr. [Thomas] Walker and other adventurous spirits, inspired the younger members of the [McAfee] family with enthusiasm and a burning desire to visit it and judge of its beauties for themselves."[5] The McAfee explorations would, as we shall see, prove to be of key importance to our story.

After a century (1670–1770) of steady immigration from Europe and the subsequent development of quiet hamlets into bustling towns, many mid-eighteenth-century citizens of the British Crown thought the King's most prized colonies had become too crowded and too overfarmed. In the minds of some colonists, the New World had become too much like the Old World of England, Scotland, Ireland, Wales, Holland, Sweden, Switzerland, or Germany, the places they had left behind. Though 90 percent of the colonists during that period were farmers, the desire of the restless and the disgruntled to push westward into the fabled region the British called "Indian Reserve" became a clarion call in churches, taverns, and meeting halls from the late 1690s into the first half of the 1700s.

By the 1750s and 1760s, the focus of further colonial exploration had turned to locating suitable regions for settlement. The lushness of the Bluegrass held particular attraction to the surveyors. One notable surveyor, Christopher Gist, wrote in 1751 with evident excitement as he approached the Kentucky River, "From the top of the Mountain we saw fine level country SW as far as our Eyes could behold, and it was a clear Day." Of his movements the next day, Gist wrote, ". . . at about 12 M. came to the Cuttaway [Kentucky] River; We were obliged to go up it about 1 m. to an island which was the shoalest place We coud find to cross at . . ."[6] Gist's chronicled movements suggest that the crossing he describes might be at the very location, later to be called Leestown, that lay about one mile from present-day Frankfort and was a critical part of the famed ancient buffalo trail, referred to by the native tribes as "great buffalo trace."

The Amazement, the Terror

Aside from the empty vastness and developmental potential of the western wilderness, one common impression communicated by the returning frontiersmen, especially the celebrated "longhunters" like Daniel and Squire Boone, Henry Skaggs, James Harrod, Isaac Bledsoe, Richard Callaway, and others involved their stirring firsthand accounts of the breathtaking numbers of big game creatures. Elk, whitetail deer, black bear, panther, beaver, bobcat, wolf, wolverine, wild boar, and bison reigned supreme in the frontier's dense woodlands, bogs, limestone outcroppings, plains, and meadows. Even allowing for the seasonal hunting by the regional tribes, big game populations of unimaginable sizes flourished in the region that now encompasses all or part of the heartland states of Kentucky, Tennessee, Ohio, Indiana, Michigan, and Illinois.

But of all the recorded accounts concerning big game, the most indelible impressions were spun courtesy of the horned, cocoa-brown-colored, and aggressive American bison. Zoology long ago determined that the two distinct varieties of buffalo in the greater Bovid family had for millennia been found solely in sub-Saharan Africa (the ornery and dangerous Cape buffalo) and southeastern Asia (the water buffalo), and not in North America until relatively recently. Buffalo and bison are related but biologically different. DNA findings from bones excavated in northern Canada suggest, however, that bison herds emigrated from eastern Asia anywhere from 195,000 to 130,000 years ago, traveling over the natural Bering Straits land bridge that connected eastern Asia to Alaska. The buffalo cousins that made the journey, two Bovid families of bison, are divided between the American bison and the European bison. Nevertheless, the English- and French-speaking explorers of the western frontier from their initial seventeenth century portrayals referred to the American bison by a variety of names, including *biffalo, bofelo, buffalow, bufflo, buffaloe,* and, most commonly, *buffalo.* That latter sobriquet, though technically incorrect, has endured to the present day. In keeping with this quirky custom, I will refer to the American bison as *buffalo* moving forward.

In terms of individual size the North American buffalo is an imposing, sinewy yet compact biological machine. Females average from 700 to 1,000 pounds, stand five feet at the shoulder and are six to seven feet from nose to tail while males can tip the scales at 1,800 to 2,000 pounds, stand six feet at the shoulder and span up to nine feet in length. In their innate "fight or flight" genetic programming, the slightest disturbance while they are at rest or grazing can, in an instant, set an entire herd into unpredictable, helter-skelter motion from zero to 30 miles per hour. This hair-trigger reflex is why Native American hunters, who regarded the buffalo as a sacred being, used so much caution, stealth, and concealing costumes when in the hunt. Their elaborate precautions taught the Euro-American longhunters and their successors about the necessity for extreme safeguard measures when dealing with the skittish buffaloes.

The Euro-American explorers encountered buffalo not only in small groups of 20 to 50 but also in vast herds in the tens of thousands, stretching across middle America's fertile prairies, which were carpeted with swaying short and tall grasses. The largest reported gatherings ranged from 100 to 500,000 buffalo. As the massive herds of buffalo trotted in migration mode, the ground underfoot quaked in rolling temblors and the air hummed with the sound of hooved thunder and guttural murmurs. The pong of hide, urine, and dung stung the eyes and clouds of billowing dust clogged the nostrils. Witnessing wild buffalo searching for sustenance in such staggering numbers proved such an awe-inspiring spectacle that it inspired the more literate early adventurers to connect pen to notebook. "The amazing herds of buffaloes, which resort thither, by their size and number, fill the traveller with amazement and terrors, especially when he beholds the prodigious roads they have made from all quarters as if leading to some populous city," described Kentucky surveyor, mapmaker, historian, and pioneer John Filson in 1784.[7] Twenty-one years later on August 29, 1806, William Clark wrote in the journal of his historic expedition to the Pacific Ocean with Meriwether Lewis about the spectacle of the buffalo population, estimated then to be in the range of at least 30 million, and by some estimates possibly 60 million, across the continent. Of the wonder he felt, Clark wrote, "I assended to the high Country and from an eminance I had a view of the plains for a great distance. From this eminance I had a view of a greater number of buffalow than I had ever Seen before at one time. I must have Seen near 20,000 of those animals feeding on this plain."[8]

The buffalo herds were perpetually in motion. They thrived by grazing on the nutrient-rich, flat-as-a-tabletop, grassy plains, and sheltered in woodland regions that spanned from northwestern Canada south through the heartland prairies to northern Mexico, as well as southeast to the hardwood forests of the Appalachian mountain chain. The immense range that sustained the buffalo population covered more than one-third of the North American continent in the late 1500s. Buffalo roamed unchallenged throughout this vast tract of North America, trampling and sculpting the terrain and flora by the sheer enormity of their numbers and the incessant pounding of millions of hooves. Their seasonal migrations traveled along ancient pathways that had been carved into the landscape over millennia. Many of the buffalo trails, or *traces*, were in some locations hundreds of feet wide and up to four feet deep. Their battered traces in which the dirt was pulverized to an almost stone-like hardness were connected, like the blue highways on a present-day roadmap, by specific locations and topographical intersections that provided natural mineral deposits, such as sulfur, magnesium, calcium, phosphorus, potassium, and sodium chloride. The most important mineral deposit of all to the herds, more vital than all the other minerals, was sodium chloride (NaCl), also known as salt.

Salt is a key life-sustaining nutrient for all of the Earth's marine and terrestrial mammals. Sodium chloride is vital to the daily maintenance of muscle and nerve function, as well as fluid regulation. When mammals, including humans, sweat and urinate, they lose sodium. Mammals that reside in the planet's oceans, like dolphins, whales, otters, seals, walruses, and porpoises, are surrounded by salt, so their replenishment of sodium is easily met. Land-based mammals, however, must by necessity search for salt. This is especially true of the large, four-legged mammals that inhabit the continental landmasses.

Early visitors in the Ohio River Valley soon learned that the resting spots of mammal herds connected by traces served as roadway markers for their constant roaming in search of edible vegetation, salt, and fresh water. One observant geographer, Gilbert Imlay, described in the 1790s one of these mineral-laden stations, scribbling, "A salt spring is called a 'Lick' from the earth about them being furrowed out in a most curious manner by the buffalo and deer, which lick the earth on account of the saline particles with which it is impregnated."[9] Another eyewitness account from the late 1790s whose author remains unknown depicted the effect of groups of buffaloes, writing, "The vast space of land around the salt springs desolated as by a ravaging enemy and the hills reduced to plains by the pawing of their feet. I have heard a hunter assert that he saw about a thousand buffaloes at the Blue Licks in Kentucky at one time."

Prior to the invasion of travelers from the British colonies to northern Kentucky via avenues like the Wilderness Trail, the Cumberland Gap, and the Ohio River, native tribes utilized the roads bulldozed by buffalo herds as trade, warring, and hunting routes. An account from one of Reverend James Smith's trio of journals from 1783, 1795, and 1797 describing his travels through northern Kentucky's Bluegrass identifies one of the most famous buffalo traces, named *Atlanant-o-wamiowee* by the Shawnees. "We left the lick [probably Lower Blue Lick] and pursued our journey to Lexington following one of the old buffalo roads, which I suppose was generally 200 feet wide."[10]

From British Indian agent George Croghan's journals, dated from 1750 to 1765, came these observations, "We went to the great lick . . . On our way we passed through a fine timbered clear wood; we came into a large road which the buffaloes have beaten, spacious enough for two wagons to go abreast, and leading straight to the lick."[11] Tennessee historian and lawyer Edward Albright wrote later in the late nineteenth century, "To the licks in the region . . . came at regular intervals the animals from all over a large territory, and these in their journeys to and fro formed beaten paths or trails, all centering in this locality like the spokes of a wheel . . . all traces led to central licks . . . Hunters, both Indian and white, roaming at will through the forests came upon these narrow paths, and turning about threaded them together."[12]

As a result of these and other accounts, names were bestowed on salt licks to identify their locations: French Lick, Big Lick, Licking Creek, White Lick, Big Bone Lick, Lower Blue Lick, Drennan's Lick, Knob Lick, May's Lick. The network of buffalo traces, connected by mineral salt licks, was the American heartland's first super-highway system. It provided a reliable web of terrestrial arteries that guided many of the bands of eastern colonists who yearned for the wider spaces, more fertile lands, and more abundant hunting grounds that lay west of the Appalachian Mountains. Some traces were busier than others, due mostly to their advantageous crossings at significant rivers and streams or their proximity to major salt deposits. As homesteaders with building and farming skills followed the explorers and surveyors in the last quarter of the 1700s, villages, merchant outposts, inns, and way stations mushroomed along traces in northern Kentucky, northern Tennessee, southern Ohio, and southern Indiana.

In 1968, John A. Jakle, assistant professor of geography at the University of Illinois, composed a comprehensive paper, titled *The American*

Bison and The Human Occupance of the Ohio Valley.[13] One passage from Mr. Jakle's document is particularly pertinent to this book, as it reads, "The Atlanant-o-wamiowee crossed into Kentucky at the mouth of the Licking River, proceeded south to Big Bone and Drennon's Licks, cut east to the Great Buffalo Crossing at present-day Frankfort, and continued via Lower Blue and May's Licks to the Limestone Crossing." In the complex Shawnee language, an offshoot of the Central Algonquin tongue, *Atlanant-o-wamiowee* means "the buffalo trace." But Mr. Jakle's most salient 10-word passage from his analysis is ". . . cut east to the Great Buffalo Crossing at present-day Frankfort . . ." Salient, for it is here at this place, the low trough of sandy bank and animal crossing on the Kentucky River, just a healthy stone's throw from what would become Frankfort, Kentucky, where the story of distilling in Kentucky's Bluegrass and Buffalo Trace Distillery starts.

The Unforgivable Extermination of *Tatanka*

In the pre-Columbian era, the robust North American buffalo population provided food from meat and vital organs, as well as shelter, clothing, weapons, tools, footwear, cord from hide and sinew, and fuel from dung for the native tribes that resided in the center of the continent. The nomadic Lakota, Pawnee, Kiowa, Osage, Blackfeet, Crow, Arapaho, Cherokee, Shawnee, Iroquois, Comanche, and many more tribes that followed the migrating herds of buffalo had a seemingly endless supply of basic sustenance. The native communities of the plains were, by and large, thoughtful in their relationship with the herds of *tatanka*, as the Lakota called the buffalo. For millennia, the tribes were aware that their own welfare and generational perpetuation depended almost entirely on their stewardship of the buffalo.

Everything changed for the worse starting in the late 1600s with the arrival of French, Spanish, and English hunters in North America's hinterlands. As weaponry evolved, the hunters' use of long-range, high-caliber Sharps, as well as Springfield and Remington No. 1 rifles, indiscriminately slaughtered buffalo for their hides, tongues, and horns, which were coveted in the eastern colonies and throughout Europe. Beginning around 1800, a cold-blooded, systematic extermination of buffalo conducted both by private citizens (often from the distant safety of trains or wagons) and the U.S. military brought the number of buffalo tumbling from tens of millions to less than 100 by 1883. This senseless, cold-blooded action stands as the largest case of mass murder of mammals over the span of one century in world history. The December 27, 1899, edition of the *Morning Post North Carolina* best summed up the genocidal crimes, saying, "One of the most extraordinary events that has characterized the last half of the present century is the extermination, the wiping out of the American bison . . . bones and pictures alone tell the story of a mighty race swept from the face of the earth by civilized people of the 19th century."

Most evil of all, the U.S. government backed this act of premeditated mass annihilation to punish and cripple the Native American tribal societies, instigating, along with the intentional spread of viral diseases like smallpox, the downfall of the indigenous communities that once thrived from southern Canada to northern Mexico on land they viewed as sacred. A century and a half later, the pain of the native population continues on the squalid, poverty-stricken reservations scattered around the continent that are often located far from ancestral sites.

Meanwhile, dispersed among several states, the current buffalo population ranges from 500,000 to 600,000 head in the United States. Through the tireless efforts primarily of conservationists (Wildlife Conservation Society, National Bison Association) and the Native American community (InterTribal Buffalo Council), the U.S. Congress passed a bill, the National Bison Legacy Act, proclaiming the buffalo as the national mammal. The bill was made into law with the signature of President Barack Obama on May 9, 2016. Certainly, this institutional act is to be applauded, if tepidly. In light of the despicable mass slaughter that bathed the American prairies in the blood of the nation's most celebrated four-legged mammal, it seems like cold comfort indeed.

2

"This Map of Kentucke: Drawn from Actual Observations . . ."

LEWIS EVANS OF Philadelphia was an educated man and an industrious science-minded contemporary of another commendable eighteenth-century Philadelphian, Benjamin Franklin. While Franklin applied his prodigious intellect to understanding nature, studying the frailties and strengths of humankind, and to defining how a democratic republic should function, Evans, lauded by the authors of *Degrees of Latitude: Mapping Colonial America* Margaret Beck Pritchard and Henry G. Taliaferro as "the best geographer working in the English colonies,"[1] mapped in remarkable detail the uncharted region directly to the west of the 13 established colonies. Evans's initial effort, a meticulously drawn map completed in 1755, depicted numerous firsthand observations that helped guide Euro-American explorers for decades afterward. Notations, such as the positions of Native American encampments and pioneer settlements, the navigability of rivers, limestone deposits and shelves, salt licks, the locations of hills, worn pathways, traces and roads, coal deposits, and suggested portages, were drawn with clarity and precision.

In a later, even more comprehensive version, dated 1776, Evans shows the "Kentucke" River adjacent to entries such as "A Chain of small broken hills" and "Elephants Bones found here." Evans's "elephant bones" mention, it should be noted, refers to unearthed mammoth tusks. This map shows the Kentucke River joining the Ohio River to the northwest. Evans's 1776 map remains the first known cartographical citing of the Kentucke River, on which much notable distilling history would later be made.

It is worth noting now that the official spelling of *Kentucky* with a "y" came later, around the time the territory gained statehood in 1792. Early variations on the term include *Kentucke, Kaintuckee,* and *Cantuckey.* The original name is thought to have been possibly derived from one of the Native American descriptors for the region, such as *kan-tah-the* from the Wyandotte nation or *kin-athiki* from the Algonquin tribe.

Mentioned previously in Chapter 1, John Filson was another Kentucky surveyor, journalist, and cartographer of distinction. Filson, who originally hailed from Lancaster, Pennsylvania, supplied yet another finely fashioned map of Kentucky, but years later in 1784, immediately after the conclusion of American Revolutionary War hostilities. The inscription at the top of Filson's map reads, with admirable politeness, "This map of Kentucke: drawn from actual observations, is inscribed with the most perfect respect, to the honorable congress of the United States of America, and to his Excell'cy George Washington, late commander in chief of their army. By their humble servant, John Filson. 1784."[2]

Filson's outstanding mapmaking effort had a tight, pinpoint scale of 10 miles to an inch, making it easily readable for anyone hankering to make the weeks'-long journey from the eastern colonies. Filson himself established roots near the settlement of Lexington in approximately 1782 after purchasing a sizeable parcel of land. His anecdotal book, published like his map in 1784, was titled *The Discovery, Settlement and Present State of Kentucke.* It sold for $1.50 and enjoyed but a single pressing that numbered 1,500 copies.

John Filson's 1784 map of Kentucky.   **Library of Congress**

Tragically, John Filson vanished in October of 1788 while on a surveying mission in the remote woodlands of southern Ohio. The enduring
story is that after Filson's group happened upon a small Shawnee hunting camp, a heated dispute ensued among the members of his party as to
how to approach the tribe, either peacefully or with muskets blazing. The
disagreement proved so vehement that it splintered the group into smaller

factions. In what can only be considered a lapse of sound judgment, the frustrated Filson wandered off on his own into the depths of the forest to continue his surveying mission. Like so many men and women of his time, John Filson was never heard from again and his body was never found.[3]

Adventurers from the New England colonies tended to explore the virgin region north of the Ohio River, the expansive Great Lakes area of present-day Ohio, Indiana, Illinois, Michigan, and Wisconsin, termed the Northwest Territory. By contrast, Evans, Filson, and other survey-ors from Virginia and North Carolina colonies, most prominently, John Floyd, James Douglas, William Preston, and Isaac Hite, served genera-tions of travelers by furnishing the logistical tools via their cartographic and journalistic data for the inevitable settlement of northern Kentucky. Small wonder, then, that after the signing of the Treaty of Fort Stanwix in October 1768 between Great Britain and the Six Nations of the Iroquois Confederation, relinquishing what is now much of Kentucky to the Brit-ish Crown, settlers in Virginia Colony began packing their wagons, oxen, packhorses, and mules. This fateful treaty, signed by Sir William Johnson and the Iroquois chiefs, gave license to colonists to venture, at least theo-retically, unfettered into the far western sections of Pennsylvania, New York, and Virginia. The treaty's contents included western Virginia's Fin-castle County, in what is now most of Kentucky. One of the Fort Stanwix treaty's glaring shortcomings, however, included the exclusion from the agreement of the Shawnee and Cherokee nations, two important non-Iroquois tribes of approximately 4,000 and 10,000 people, respectively. This omission would, in part, be the cause of fatal trouble down the road. From 1750 to 1785, thousands of colonial travelers trudged westward across Pennsylvania Colony to faraway Fort Pitt, original site of the city of Pittsburgh. Built by the British from 1759 to 1761 during the French and Indian War at the confluence of the Monongahela and Alleghany rivers, Fort Pitt proved to be the ideal launching point onto the frontier's west-southwest leading aquatic superhighway, the Ohio River.

Other seekers for adventure, riches, and new horizons, including Daniel Boone and his comrades, walked, rode a mule or horse, or drove bumpy, two-wheel buckboards through the Cumberland Gap, a naturally formed V-shaped passage sliced through the Appalachian Mountains.

The renowned Cumberland Gap is located near what today is the state border between Virginia to the east and Kentucky to the northwest. Many male pilgrims journeyed west in the late 1760s and early 1770s via the Gap to find the parcels of land granted to them via the Royal Proclamation of October 7, 1763, by the final Royal Governor of Virginia Colony, John Murray, fourth Earl of Dunmore. The land grants, from a total of 172,850 acres of available land, were payment for their military service to the British Crown during the French and Indian War (1754–1763). Such land-as-compensation arrangements were commonplace at the time, due primarily to the colonial government's inability to pay soldiers in currency for their time in uniform on behalf of the British Crown. Undeveloped land was plentiful and strongly desired in the 1760s.

This active period of movement in the early second half of the eighteenth century was pivotal, as we shall see, in setting in motion the saga of Buffalo Trace Distillery. On May 10, 1773, the five members of the McAfee Company, James, George, and Robert McAfee along with John McCoun and James Pawling, made their way west from Botetourt County, Virginia, into the verdant Bluegrass region for the purpose of finding suitable land on which to settle. Soon after reaching the 97-mile long Kanawha River in what is now West Virginia, the three McAfees dispatched McCoun and Pawling back to their Virginia homesteads with their mounts and encountered Hancock Taylor's group of surveyors. Taylor, like so many other commissioned surveyors, was en route to traverse the Ohio River westward to its joining with the Mississippi River, exploring the adjacent countryside along the way. Together on June 1, 1773, at the mouth of the Kanawha, the McAfees and Taylor met up with Thomas Bullitt, who led a large contingent of 40 men for the Ohio Land Company.[4] Bullitt's mission was likewise to sail down the Ohio River looking for suitable places on which to build outposts and defensive blockhouses. For reasons of safe passage and shared information, the three companies allied, creating a formidable armada with more than 50 able-bodied men. They floated down the tricky currents of the Ohio River in bark canoes and crude pirogues, or dugouts. Once the flotilla reached the mouth of Limestone Creek, later to become the settlement of Maysville, Kentucky, Robert McAfee, against cries of sibling protest, strode off alone to explore on foot the riverside expanse on the Ohio's desolate south bank. After days of exhausting solo exploration, traveling with deliberation west/southwest along the rocky banks of the Ohio, McAfee, in full possession of his scalp, rejoined his brothers, Hancock Taylor, and Thomas Bullitt at the mouth of the 303-mile-long Licking River.[5]

Days later, the trio of companies beached where the Kentucky River merged with the much larger Ohio. There on July 4, 1773, Hancock Taylor and the McAfees separated from Thomas Bullitt's Ohio Land Company after deciding instead to paddle their pirogues laden with flour, gunpowder, beans, and salted pork up the placid, 259-mile-long Kentucky River in search of suitable terrain to survey for homesteading. Meanwhile, Bullitt and his party continued on their westward journey down the wide Ohio River.

Following days of slow exploration negotiating the numerous blind twists and hairpin turns of the Kentucky River, the McAfees and Taylor on July 16 waded across the shallows, probably a sandbar, to a low-banked spot that was doubtless a broad, beaten-down buffalo trace. The men hiked up the gentle incline through billowing clouds of fine dust to view an elevated bottomland pasture that was fragrant with white clover, bluegrass, and buffalo grass. This locale would later become the settlement of the city of Frankfort. Using the day's topographers' tools, primarily compasses and Gunter's chains, the legally recognized metal-linked measuring devices, James and Robert McAfee and Hancock Taylor surveyed plots of land in sizes of hundreds of acres for the future settlement of the McAfee family in what was then still considered Fincastle County, Virginia.

What they didn't know in the sweaty mid-July heat and humidity of 1773 was that their comrade, Hancock Taylor, would one year later, in late July 1774, be shot by hostile Native Americans and die of his wounds on August 1. Taylor in 1774 was, like Thomas Bullitt, surveying for the Ohio Land Company. He was surveying near the great buffalo trace when the rifle shot that would kill him rang out from among the woodland shadows. Taylor's cousin, Willis Lee, accompanied him on that Kentucky River survey. With Willis Lee's initial presence in 1774 at that precise location, the course of that site's history would forever be altered. One year later, in 1775, Willis Lee and his brother Captain Hancock Lee III, a civil engineer, plotted out the first mappings of what would become Leestown.

The Birth of Leestown and the Gift of "a Rattlesnake skin"

The family roots of brothers Hancock III and Willis Lee, the founders of Leestown, are believed to go back to the time of William the Conqueror in eleventh-century Europe. One family account, recorded in 1903 in the *Register of the Kentucky State Historical Society*, claims that Launcelot Lee of Lourdes, France, ". . .was a trusted officer of William the Conqueror when he went on that wonderful free-booting [looting] expedition to England."[6] Most probably in the late 1600s or early 1700s, Launcelot Lee's descendants made their way from Great Britain to the New World, settling in Northumberland County, Virginia. Existing historical records do not disclose whether they "wonderfully free-booted" across the Atlantic Ocean. The eighteenth-century Lee brothers were the offspring of Hancock II and Mary Willis Lee.

Brothers Hancock and Willis Lee were hardly the first colonial land speculators to set foot upon the great buffalo trace crossing site, as various accounts show that other adventurers preceded the Lees across its shoals. They were the pioneers, however, whose reconnoiters bore the most fruitful consequences. The great buffalo trace crossing was one of the few low spots along the otherwise steeply banked Kentucky River, making its location advantageous. A topographical assessment dated from 1794 confirmed this, saying, "The banks of Kentucky River are remarkably high; in some places 300 and 400 feet, composed generally of stupendous perpendicular rock; the consequence is, there are few crossing places; the best is at Leestown. . ."[7]

Among the earliest Euro-American surveyors to disturb the ankle-deep dust of the great buffalo trace were the previously cited Dr. Thomas Walker and Christopher Gist, who in 1750–1751 visited the Bluegrass on behalf of the Ohio Land Company. The breakout in 1754 of the French and Indian War, with the British combating the French and their native tribal allies for nine blood-soaked years, made exploratory excursions through Fincastle County hazardous up to the mid-1760s. Other pre–Lee era explorers to pass along this route included fur traders and friends John Findley and Daniel Boone in 1766–1767. By 1770–1772, the Shawnee and Cherokee hunting parties that routinely used the crossing encountered, with disturbing regularity, the footprints made by colonials' leather boots. Yet the dogged persistence of the Euro-Americans to explore and settle the Bluegrass continued in the same vein as a relentless horror film monster that just keeps coming, no matter how many times it is blasted with gunfire.

In June of 1774, former Pennsylvanian James Harrod, accompanied by 37 men, founded Harrods Town (the name was later changed to Harrodsburg), 39 miles to the west of the Kentucky River. Harrodsburg was the initial stockade community to be founded in Kentucky. Less than one year later in April 1775 at a site located 48 miles to the east of Harrodsburg, a group of 30-plus axmen, led by Daniel Boone, established Fort Boone, later renamed Boonesborough. This settlement was established after the troop hacked a trail through the woodlands with a starting point at Long Island of the Holston in eastern Tennessee. Likewise in 1775, Benjamin Logan founded St. Asaph (a.k.a. Logan's Fort and later to become Stanford, Kentucky) situated to the south of Leestown by roughly 60 miles. In 1776, the Virginia legislature introduced the wonderfully named Corn Patch and Cabin Rights Act that promised ownership of 400 acres in the untamed District of Kentucky to anyone willing to brave the weeks'-long journey to erect a log cabin, cultivate corn in Virginia's westernmost region, and survive the attacks by tribal war parties.

British explorer Nicholas Cresswell provided one of the more striking accounts of life on the Kentucky River through his daily journal, written in the years 1774–1777. In several passages from 1775, Cresswell addressed the presence of the Lee brothers in the vicinity of the site of present-day Buffalo Trace Distillery. Cresswell's account on May 23, 1775, reads as follows, "Proceeded up the [Kentucky] River, found several rapids which obliged us to get out and haul our vessel up with ropes. The current stronger than yesterday. Saw several roads that crossed the River which they tell me were made by the Buffaloes going from one lick to another. (These licks are brackish or salt springs which the Buffaloes are fond of.)"

The next day, May 24, Cresswell wrote, "Camped at a place where the Buffaloes cross the River. In the night were alarmed with a plunging in the River . . . found one of our Canoes that had all our flour on board sunk . . . It was done by the Buffaloes crossing the River . . ." Then on Sunday, June 11, 1775, Cresswell reported, "This morning killed a Buffalo Cow crossing the River. Fell down to Elkhorn Creek . . . Found Captn. Hancock Lee camped at Elkhorn, surveying land . . . I believe the land is good in general, through the whole track, with several salt springs as I am informed. An immense number of Buffaloes frequent them. Buffaloes are a sort of wild cattle but have a large hump on the top of their shoulders all black, and their necks and shoulders covered with long shaggy hair with large bunches of hair growing on their fore thighs, short horns bending forward, short noses, piercing eyes and beard like a goat . . . They do not roar like other cattle, but grunt like hogs. Got a large pine canoe out of some drift wood with great labour . . . Excessively hot."

Finally on Monday, June 12, Cresswell wrote, "Went to Captn. Lee's camp, who treated me very kindly with a dram of Whiskey and some bread, which at this time is a great luxury with me. Captn. Lee's brother [Willis] gave me a Rattlesnake skin about four feet long."[8] Presumably, Lee had, of course, carried the whiskey from his starting point in Virginia and had not distilled it while on the road.

Hancock Lee's camp on Elkhorn Creek was but four miles as the crow flies east of the great buffalo trace crossing on the Kentucky River. Soon after their encounter with Nicholas Cresswell, he and Willis turned their attention back to the crossing site to plot their own family settlement. A deputy surveyor, George Rogers Clark, who worked under Captain Hancock Lee described the site with obvious gusto in a letter, dated, "Lees Town, Kentucke, July 6th, 1775," to his brother Jonathan that said, ". . . A richer and more beautiful country than this I believe has never been seen in America . . . We have laid out a town seventy miles up ye Kentucke where I intend to live, and I don't doubt that there will be fifty families living in it by Christmas."[9] From this and other descriptions of the crossing, it is simple to understand why the Lees, following the surveys of the McAfees and Hancock Taylor two years earlier, decided to build their initial log lean-tos and storage shelters right there at that spot. "Lying in a sharp bend of the river, near a shallow ford of shelving rock, with a spacious sandy beach on which to land and load or unload canoes and other boats, and with never-failing springs of cold, pure water near at hand, with a large natural meadow in easy reach and a rich bottom of level land sufficiently extensive to provide the settlers with an abundant supply of corn, and with broad buffalo roads radiating to the East and West, it is by no means surprising that this particular spot had attracted the eye of Robert McAfee and Hancock Taylor and was afterwards chosen by Hancock Lee as the site for his town," addressed Kentucky historian Judge Samuel M. Wilson in his remarks at the 1931 dedication of a marker at the Leestown site. Wilson's speech, titled, *Leestown – Its Founders and Its History*, was recorded in the Register of the Kentucky State Historical Society.[10]

On December 27, 1775, Hancock Lee III registered a number of parceled claims in Fincastle County, Virginia, totaling 2,800 acres, with 1,200 acres relating specifically to Leestown. One parcel of 400 acres was described by Lee as being at the "Great Buffalow crossing on Cedar Creek." Additional claims by Willis and Richard Lee, most adjoining Leestown, secured a significant area of land. In all, the Lees claimed 8,800 acres, the majority in and around Leestown, and smaller plots near Elkhorn Creek.

But, regrettably, the euphoria of the brothers' companion George Rogers Clark and the Lees' own ambitions concerning Leestown collided head-on with the sobering realities of wilderness habitation in northern Kentucky in the last quarter of the eighteenth century. The region's struggling remaining native tribes, specifically the Shawnees and their Iroquois-speaking allies, the Mingos, shared neither the joy nor the optimism of the Lees and their party. Tribal leaders viewed the establishment of Leestown and the other meager compounds in the Bluegrass as aggressive encroachments on their traditional hunting grounds. The founding of populated compounds and deforested fields by the colonials disturbed and reduced the numbers of the game animals. Worse still, the callous murder of a local tribal chief's family members by a throng of Euro-American settlers in 1774 as well as a string of broken treaties with the British likewise fanned the flames of vengeance. Also in 1774, the Battle of Point Pleasant, pitting Virginia Colony militias against the warriors of the Shawnee and Mingo tribes in what is now West Virginia, ended badly for the Shawnees and Mingos. After the fight, the tribes agreed to relinquish their rights to all lands west of the North Carolina and Virginia colonies. This included all of the District of Kentucky.

Thus, amidst the festering rancor between the native tribes and the Euro-Americans, in April of 1776 catastrophe struck when a band of Mingo warriors waded across the great buffalo trace armed with tomahawks and bows and arrows, and rifles and attacked Leestown. In the hand-to-hand skirmish Willis Lee was killed and resident Cyrus McCracken was badly wounded. The few crude log cabins and storage sheds were set ablaze. Leaving their bulky possessions and the incapacitated Willis Lee behind, the handful of ambulatory settlers fled Leestown, scrambling their way through miles of dense forest and across open pasture to the relative safety of Boonesborough. Some historians have viewed the shooting of Hancock Taylor that occurred two years earlier in the same light of tribal retribution. Whatever the case, with shocking abruptness, any sense of secure occupancy at the river landing christened Leestown was shattered. Even though this single attack could hardly be characterized as a major battle when compared to other confrontations, the ferocity and swiftness of its nature became the topic of conversation that planting season at every campfire and fortified homestead in the Bluegrass. Consequently, the Shawnee and Mingo tribes were demonized, making them the targets of the subsequent wrath of the Euro-American settlers.

From the mid-1770s to the early 1780s, the severity and number of the hostilities between settlers and the agitated native tribes made passage throughout the Bluegrass untenable. Blood-curdling tales of the horrendous tortures, including being burned or skinned alive or of having ears, noses, and limbs severed, suffered by the unfortunate pioneers who were captured by tribal war parties dominated the conversations within the settlements. To make matters worse, with the Revolutionary War raging at an all-hands-on-deck degree all along the eastern seaboard, no militias could be roused to help defend the western frontier against the stealthy sorties of the native warriors.

Indeed, many pioneers, including Hancock Lee, who served in one of the nine companies of troops of the 13th Virginia Regiment, returned to the eastern colonies to fight the British, a move that further depleted the manpower of the western frontier settlements. Consequently, Fincastle County's four vulnerable and lightly armed communities – Leestown, Boonesborough, St. Asaphs, and Harrodsburg – were left to fend for themselves until the end of the Revolutionary War. In their book *A New History of Kentucky*, authors Lowell H. Harrison and James C. Klotter write, "By late spring 1776 the pioneer population of Kentucky was estimated to be no more than 200, and most of these people were in forts . . . By early 1778 Kentucky had by one count only 121 able-bodied riflemen . . . in a total population of about 280."[11] Following the 1776 raid and with Hancock Lee's departure to serve in the war, Leestown was likely abandoned throughout the duration of the war. Yet even in the wake of the 1776 assault by the Mingo warriors and the lack of population, Leestown remained on the county register for its strategic commercial potential as a suitable future river landing. The local Land Court, for example, notes its existence in 1779–1780 when no one may have been in residence at the great buffalo trace.

By the autumn of 1781, the Revolutionary War started to wind down as the battlefield tide turned against the crumbling and cash-poor British war machine. The surrender of General Charles Cornwallis to General George Washington at Yorktown in October 1781 proved to be the first toppling domino. Twenty-three months later, in September of 1783, the war officially concluded with the signing of the Treaty of Paris. Continental Army veterans and militia members alike began returning to the Bluegrass to reclaim their homesteads and resume their agrarian livelihoods. Hancock Lee traveled back to revive Leestown, and he wasted no time in making progress.

In 1783, legislation in the Virginia General Assembly allowed Hancock Lee to build a warehouse, declaring, ". . . the erection of a warehouse for the inspection of tobacco, in the county of Fayette [formerly Fincastle], at Leestown, on the Kentucky River, on the lands of Hancock Lee, will be of public benefit . . ."[12] Whether Lee's actual warehouse was ever erected that year at the great buffalo trace even with the blessing of the Virginia General Assembly remains unclear. A previous log structure, referred to as a "blockhouse," was erected sometime after the Mingo raid of 1776 more as a means of defense than of stock storage. Later county records do prove beyond the shadow of a doubt, however, that warehouses were built in time as Leestown's prime low-bank location served it well as a commercial depot on the bustling Kentucky River in the late eighteenth and early nineteenth centuries. Hancock Lee, meanwhile, was the recipient of good news about three years after his return from the war. He was bestowed clear title in 1786 to the land claims that he had inherited from his cousin Hancock Taylor and his brother Willis after their tragic murders. This legal action solidified Hancock's control of the plot on which Leestown was built.

But even with such an advantageous position on the bank of a major tributary of the Ohio River, Leestown stayed little more than a modest municipality, dotted with a few cabins and small warehouses made of logs. Its positional strength was as a serviceable river landing, but not necessarily as a desirable residential location. The ravages of the war in the east altered the directions of peoples' lives in the west. George Rogers Clark, Lee's deputy surveyor, for example, never returned to Leestown despite his earlier declarations, later settling in what would become the state of Ohio after leading troops in the violent Indian Wars (1775–1783). Leestown's population thus remained small while other nearby communities grew.

Then later in 1786, a blustery tornado twisted and corkscrewed its way through the Bluegrass. That storm had a name. General James Wilkinson. And with Wilkinson's appearance, life in Leestown would be forever changed.

3

"...As Crooked as a Dog's Hind Leg..."

In 1894, FUTURE U.S. president and then New York governor Theodore Roosevelt minced no words in his searing assessment of the personality of General James Wilkinson, writing in his book *The Winning of the West: From the Alleghenies to the Mississippi*, "In character, he [Wilkinson] can only be compared to Benedict Arnold, though he entirely lacked Arnold's ability and brilliant courage. He had no conscience and no scruples; he had not the slightest idea of the meaning of the word honor . . . In all our history there is no more despicable character."[1] Noted early twentieth-century historian of the western United States Frederick Jackson Turner, author of the essay *Frontier Thesis: The Significance of the Frontier in American History* (1893), accused Wilkinson of being "the most consummate artist in treason the nation has ever possessed."[2] As if those words of condemnation composed long after Wilkinson's death in 1825 weren't enough, in 1908, Alfred Henry Lewis, the author of *An American Patrician, or The Story of Aaron Burr*, piled on, depicting Wilkinson via a supposed conversation between Burr and a Samuel Swartwout as being ". . . as crooked as a dog's hind leg."[3]

So then, aside from being an alleged colossal falsifier of facts, a purported traitor, and a notorious scoundrel, who was James Wilkinson? And, further, what bearing did Wilkinson and his flamboyant exploits have on the flight path of Buffalo Trace Distillery and its surrounding community?

Born in Maryland Colony in 1757, the exuberant James Wilkinson rose rapidly through guile, charm, a quick wit, and alleged dishonesty in the ranks of the Continental Army. To the consternation of many fellow officers who were more deserving and longer serving, Wilkinson became a brigadier general at the age of 20. He served, perhaps tellingly, for a short period in Canada as an aide under the American general and eventual traitor Benedict Arnold. The infamous Arnold, of course, later commanded the strategically vital fortress at West Point, which overlooked the Hudson River in New York, before defecting to join the British forces in 1780. Arnold's betrayal, which involved his planned surrender of West Point and thereby critical control of the Hudson River to the British, was heightened by the fact that he eventually fought against the American forces he once commanded.

Leaving Arnold's command in August 1776, Wilkinson then served as an aide to the well-respected general of the Continental Army, Horatio Gates. When General Gates sent Wilkinson on a time-sensitive mission to update Congress with official dispatches concerning the victory of American forces over the British at the Battle of Saratoga, Wilkinson famously kept the anxious members of Congress waiting reportedly for hours while he tended to his own private affairs in Philadelphia. Later on, he was involved in an unsuccessful conspiracy and cabal to oust George Washington as supreme commander of the Continental Army. Wilkinson's plan to replace Washington with Horatio Gates crumbled in failure as support for such a treacherous action disappeared. Appalled and outraged, General Gates forced his wayward aide to resign. But somehow through his disarming demeanor, unshakable self-confidence, and cunning, Wilkinson was able to maintain his army career until he was again forced to resign his later commission in 1781 when he ineffectively served as clothier-general to the army.

Once the Revolutionary War ended and with his checkered army career reduced to gossip fodder, Wilkinson looked westward toward the frontier. Though strapped for cash, Wilkinson looked to launch a new life chapter in a region where he was unknown and where the status of being a retired general would impress the unsuspecting. According to the superb biography of Wilkinson written by Andro Linklater, titled *An Artist in Treason: The Extraordinary Double Life of General James Wilkinson*, "Despite having limited funds at his disposal, within three months Wilkinson had bought 12,550 acres on the Kentucky River and filed claims for another 18,000 acres at the Falls of the Ohio, the future Louisville . . ."[4] Included in the Kentucky River parcels were 260 prime pastureland acres, strategically positioned one mile above Leestown on the north side of the river. Wilkinson called the settlement "Frankfort," a gesture said to be in homage to the slain pioneer Stephen Frank, who years earlier had been the unfortunate victim of a native war party raid on a salt-boiling group along the Kentucky River. The spot of the attack, a shallow crossing, was originally dubbed "Frank's Ford" after the assault.

In 1791, Wilkinson returned to military activity by leading a band of Kentucky militiamen to the Northwest Territory north of the Ohio River to help combat the restive and rampaging native tribes in the ferocious Indian War. The Northwest Territory was still in shock from the nightmare of the Battle of the Wabash, an epic military disaster that was fought near the headwaters of the Wabash River in the morning mists of November 4, 1791. Over 1,000 Delaware, Wyandot, Shawnee, and Kickapoo warriors were led by three seasoned and wily warrior chiefs: Little Turtle, Blue Jacket, and Buckongahelas. For four desperate hours, the native warriors brutally destroyed, hacked, scalped, gutted, and shot a panicked, undisciplined army of ill-equipped and untested journeyman soldiers. The resounding defeat, considered to be one the most savage battles in North American history, left only 24 white soldiers unscathed, out of 1,000 officers, scouts, and soldiers. It remains the biggest, most famous victory of Native Americans over Euro-Americans in history. After his time serving in the Indian War, James Wilkinson departed from the army, this time with the rank of lieutenant colonel, commandant of the Second U.S. Infantry.

Wilkinson's mission in founding Frankfort with its close proximity to the key river landing at Leestown was twofold. First, he wanted to become the region's singular political powerhouse and arbiter. Second, Wilkinson longed to create a base of operations from which he hoped to make a fortune by wheeling and dealing his way through trade and commercial shipping agreements that pitted the American and Spanish governments against each other. Prior to the Louisiana Purchase when the United States doubled its size by buying the Louisiana Territory from France in 1803, the immense tract and its key highway, the Mississippi River, were controlled by Spain. In an audacious effort to have Kentucky secede from the United States in order to join the territory controlled by Spain, Wilkinson plotted and manufactured a dangerous game of treachery, spying, and double-dealing. To help grease the tracks for his negotiations between the new United States and Spain, Wilkinson secretly renounced his American citizenship in 1787, thereby swearing allegiance to the Spanish Crown, led by His Catholic Majestic Carlos IV. His nerve knowing no boundaries, he even persuaded the Spanish Crown to grant him a pension.

Wilkinson's acts of duplicity occurred at a fragile time of heightened tensions between the young, awash-in-debt United States of America and Spain because the Spanish had stationed a significant number of troops in places that, according to the 1803 agreement of the Louisiana Purchase, belonged to the United States. By wearing one hat as the architect of Frankfort, a representative of Kentucky, and a former officer of the U.S. military, and another hat doing business under the table on behalf of the Spanish crown, James Wilkinson, for all intents and purposes, was acting as a double agent. Incredibly and as stark proof of his narcissism, he even invented the code name "Agent 13" for himself under which he conducted his nefarious business and geopolitical dealings for the Spanish. Wilkinson's clandestine relationship with Spain was investigated by no less than four official inquiries conducted by the U.S. government. He later became involved with the War of 1812, remarkably serving once more as Major General, though his tour of duty was tainted and undermined by backroom whispers of more unpatriotic and duplicitous behavior.

Eventually, Wilkinson vacated Kentucky and was named as U.S. Envoy to Mexico. He died in 1825. He was, not surprisingly for him, buried in Mexico City, not Frankfort, not Maryland, not anywhere with an American address. As much as his founding of the city of Frankfort, Kentucky, Wilkinson's penchant for double-crossing behavior, chicanery, and self-absorption colored his legacy in bright, rainbow-like hues. Today, the city of Frankfort is not shy about telling his story, even if it is a somewhat sanitized version. As the local magazine titled *FRANK* freely admits, "It's true, Gen. James Wilkinson was a scoundrel, but he was our scoundrel."[5]

How James Wilkinson's establishment of Frankfort, the municipality where Buffalo Trace Distillery resides today just off Wilkinson Boulevard, affected Buffalo Trace Distillery is straightforward. Though as a Bluegrass municipality Leestown preceded Frankfort, its small, unsophisticated citizenry was no match for Wilkinson's style of major-league conniving, backroom dealing, and unbridled ambition. After a storehouse was at last built in Leestown, Wilkinson erected his own warehouse and started a ferry service across the Kentucky River, which curtailed traffic to Leestown's ferry. When Kentucky was granted statehood as the 15th state on June 1, 1792, Frankfort was named its capital, besting Leestown, Lexington, Danville, and Harrodsburg, even though the well-respected Hancock Lee had lobbied hard on behalf of Leestown.

In 1794, Frankfort opened its own post office; Leestown never had one. As Wilkinson grew Frankfort into the prominent business community of the Bluegrass next to the city of Lexington, even designing Frankfort's downtown district, Leestown merchants battled to stay relevant. "Leestown was long an important stopping-place for those traveling on the Kentucky River," wrote Judge Samuel Wilson in 1931, "but it is evident the building of public roads, which, for one cause or another, failed to follow the old 'Buffalo trace,' the establishment of Frankfort by General Wilkinson, in 1786, as so near and formidable a rival, with the consequent diversion of travel and traffic, detracted seriously from the growth of Leestown."[6]

Yet, in the interest of fairness, not all of James Wilkinson's follies concerning Frankfort placed Leestown at a disadvantage. Some, for a while at least, enriched it. When Wilkinson opened up trade to New Orleans for commodities, such as tobacco, hemp, whiskey, corn, and smoked meats, for several years he shipped some of them on flatboats from the landing and warehouses at Leestown. After 1800, a factory that manufactured hemp was built at Leestown and warehouses did appear for the housing of common trade goods, including whiskey. Eventually, the powerful and influential city of Frankfort, the capital of Kentucky and the brainchild of rascal and swindler extraordinaire James Wilkinson, annexed humble Leestown. Today, National Landmark historical marker #103 in Frankfort commemorates the existence of Leestown precisely at 113 Great Buffalo Trace . . . the address today of Buffalo Trace Distillery.

4

"... 10,530 bls. Flour; 1374 Whiskey; 1984 Beef and Pork ..."

DURING THE FOUR-DECADE pre–Civil War period from 1818 to 1858, Leestown's growth inched along at a snail's pace while neighboring Frankfort's accelerated in a rabbit-with-tail-on-fire fashion. Leestown did keep busy to a degree, however, as the transportation of goods upon the regional rivers by various forms of watercraft ramped up. In the first years of the large migrations westward, river-going vessels such as flatboats and keelboats, both propelled by the muscle-power of burly men, were used to ferry colonists, livestock, and cargo from Fort Pitt downriver on the Ohio, making stops en route to the Mississippi River at the Ohio's tributaries and their outposts.

Flatboats, the level, rectangular, blunt-ended crafts built by lashing together logs, were mostly functional for one-way downstream journeys. Keelboats, designed to be sleeker and narrower and therefore more maneuverable in river currents, proved to be a technological improvement in sailing but nevertheless required the brute force of men. Both gave way in time to more streamlined ships propelled by the key transportation renovation of the period, the steam engine. The commercial exchange of goods and services from northern Kentucky via the Ohio and Mississippi rivers south to the port of New Orleans brought a satisfactory degree of prosperity to the Bluegrass river towns and villages. The building of warehouses and piers, the need for stock clerks and workmen, and the presence of merchants and bankers helped to push forward the area's economic and commercial ranking. Meanwhile, more blacksmiths, carpenters, butchers, metal workers, printers, and farmers emigrated from the eastern states, bringing with them the trade skills, ingenuity, and exuberance that energized northern Kentucky towns and counties in the first half of the nineteenth century.

Yet for the towns along the Kentucky River, including Leestown and Frankfort, a major obstacle to serious growth was that aquatic traffic was seasonal, not yearlong. Safe navigation occurred only in the winter and spring months of the year when rainfall and subsequent runoff were heaviest. Even during those damp seasons, the natural peculiarities of the winding Kentucky River that included shoals, changeable sandbars, and low-lying islands posed substantial challenges for steamboats, especially for upriver passage. As a result, the waterside warehouses, like the three-story stone warehouse at Leestown erected in 1811 by Captain Richard Taylor and Willis Atwell Lee, Willis Lee's son, fell silent from summer through fall.

To amend this prohibitive situation, in 1818 the Kentucky legislature allocated $10,000 to underwrite a study of the river's navigational issues to arrive at solutions, such as dredging channels and building locks and dams, to promote greater usage through easier passage. Captain Richard Taylor, co-owner of the Leestown warehouse, was put in charge of the section of river starting at Frankfort and ending at the point that is the confluence of the Kentucky and the Ohio rivers. To assist in justifying the project, accounts of goods maintained and shipped from several dockside warehouses were supplied to the members of the legislature. One summary of shipment and storage activity for the year 1818 specifically involving the Leestown warehouse showed evidence of a busy storage space.

One particular listing is of special interest: 1,374 barrels of whiskey. Recorded at Leestown were the following estimated amounts of exported goods, as they were precisely represented:[1]

10,530 bls. Flour	1374 whiskey
1984 beef and pork	10 hhds. Tobacco
500 bls lard	427 manufactured tobacco
1000 pieces bagging	1568 coils bale rope
7 cables	20,000 lbs. bacon
1188 boxes candles	1800 do. soap
965 reams of paper	800 kegs powder

And as for goods listed as "on hand" at Leestown, these were included:

1000 bls. flour	20 whiskey
300 beef and pork	22 hhds. Tobacco
150 bls. lard	100 manufactured tobacco
300 pieces bagging	3000 coils bale rope
1 cable	80 boxes candles

The obvious questions for our purposes must be, one, "Whose whiskey was being warehoused at Leestown?" and, two, "When was whiskey first produced at Leestown?" More on that momentarily, since I first want to close the circle on the tangential topics of steamboats and traffic on the Kentucky River.

In a related matter to the modernization of river travel occurring in October of 1818, Colonels Richard and James M. Johnson, popular Kentucky politicians and novice adventurers, set out to build a steamboat at Leestown, as reported in glowing terms by the *Kentucky Gazette*: "We hail this as the commencement of an effort which will exhibit to us the importance of the navigation of the Kentucky River, and give a new spring to the trade of this place and the central parts of the state. A few more individuals with equal industry, enterprise and public spirit, would soon teach us how to realize the advantages of our natural situation."[2]

The Johnsons' steamboat, initially named "Johnson" then later changed to "Calhoun" after John C. Calhoun, the U.S. Secretary of War, set sail from the dock at Leestown in March of 1819. The adventurous Calhoun's mission, backed by the weight of full congressional approval and financial backing, was to navigate its way in tandem with another steamboat to the river city of St. Louis and then proceed on the Missouri River to the mouth of the Yellowstone River, whereupon the site for the construction of a fort would be determined. This officially sanctioned exercise was dubbed the "Yellowstone Expedition."

The Leestown warehouse, due to its superior Kentucky River position, acted as the storage depot for at least a sizeable portion of the expedition's supplies. To exert more control over the preparation process, the Johnsons purchased Richard Taylor's interest in the stone warehouse. But fate would not be kind to this undertaking. After launching from the docks of St. Louis months behind schedule, the expedition experienced one disastrous turn of events after another, some climatic, others manmade, but all of them fatal. James Johnson's epic failure to gather ample supplies for the hundreds of crewmen in a timely and sufficient manner ended up being the prevailing criticism of the failure. The Yellowstone Expedition came to a grinding, inauspicious halt near present-day Council Bluffs, Iowa, due to a combination of crippling setbacks. These stumbling blocks included being woefully ill-prepared for the severity of the 1819–1820 Midwestern winter and suffering a rampaging breakout of scurvy that ended up taking the lives of over 200 of the 1,126 men.[3] Thus, a few short, anguishing months after it was set afloat with optimistic fanfare at St. Louis, the Yellowstone Expedition ignominiously concluded in embarrassing defeat for all involved. The brothers Johnson, as the prime ringleaders of the venture, encountered not only withering scorn from the U.S. Congress and the nation's newspapers but also faced deep financial peril since they had invested heavily in the project.

Even in light of the Yellowstone Expedition disaster, the steamboat craze along the Kentucky River did not cease with the construction and sailing of the Calhoun. Indeed, an advertisement that mentioned Leestown published in The Kentucky Reporter newspaper cited another steamboat, the *Providence*, whose owner sought cargo bound for New Orleans. The ad from the May 3, 1820, edition read, "On the first rise of the waters of the Kentucky [River], the steamer 'Providence' will leave Leestown, one mile below Frankfort, for New Orleans . . . Can carry from 150 to 200 tons."[4]

The activity of the Johnsons and others with their advocacy of the merits of the steamboat's potential, coupled with the study of improving navigation on the Kentucky River, breathed new life into the landing and the three-story stone warehouse at Leestown. But if the history has shown anything, it is that nothing, good or bad, lasts forever. The continuing money problems experienced by the Johnsons and a foreclosure notice by the Bank of Kentucky forced the brothers and Willis Atwill Lee to, at last, sell their interests in the Leestown warehouse plus four acres to Philip and Jacob Swigert in 1838. The Swigert brothers were respected Frankfort citizens and businessmen.

About the same time, the Bank of Kentucky sold other parcels of Leestown property previously owned by Captain Richard Taylor to Harrison Blanton, who already owned a sizeable chunk of Leestown acreage on which stood the brick, two-and-a-half story house, erected in 1818, called "The Beeches." As most American whiskey aficionados know, the surname *Blanton* would echo long into the future of the place situated at the great buffalo trace crossing. Whether Harrison Blanton operated a rudimentary distillery in the three-story stone warehouse or in one of the other blockhouses utilized for storage remains unclear, though unsubstantiated rumors persist to the present day that he may have dabbled in distillation. But in seeking a conclusive determination, no recorded evidence was uncovered during the research period of this book to support those rumors. The reality, in my view, was that the Leestown warehouse stored barrels of whiskey produced in other places and that fact, backed up by ledgers from several sources, served as the possible root for wishful speculation about Harrison Blanton being a distiller.

Another possibility is that in Blanton family traditions, Harrison Blanton has been viewed as a distiller because so many of his contemporaries dabbled in distilling at that time. Blanton's lengthy and impressive list of achievements as a mason, gardener, horticulturalist, quarryman, house builder, and businessman seems, however, to have left little spare time for the time-consuming, labor-intensive avocation of whiskey distilling. The bulk of Harrison's time by all accounts appears to have been spent quarrying river shelf limestone for the likes of the Old Capitol Building and working with the day's premier architects, like Gideon Shryock, to construct landmark-worthy Frankfort residences, such as Hanna House in 1817, Arrowhead in 1821, the Governor Charles Morehead house in 1833, and the Orlando Brown house in 1835. Harrison's possible role as a small-scale distiller carries with it a high probability of myth and is a matter that will not be resolved until documented proof is discovered.

So, returning to our initial question posed earlier about whose barrels of whiskey were being warehoused in the Leestown building in 1818, the existing evidence suggests the most likely answer is that the stored whiskey was produced by local farmer-distillers, but not necessarily Harrison Blanton, the Johnsons, the Taylors, or the Lees or anyone else directly associated with the Leestown buildings. But all that said, storing barrels of whiskey and producing whiskey are two wildly different activities. So let's fast-forward to December 1856 for the express purpose of answering the second question: "When was whiskey without question first produced at Leestown?"

It is in the final month of 1856 when we encounter a gentleman by the name of Daniel Swigert. He is Jacob Swigert's ambitious 23-year-old son. Daniel Swigert became the owner of a parcel of land at Leestown, which according to county records included an old stone house, a stable, and "about ten to twelve acres . . . called by the name Stoney Point."[5] This single, seemingly innocuous transaction proved momentous to Buffalo Trace Distillery's history because it was here in the closing days of 1856 where the initial, irrefutable steps that led to the first physical distillation of whiskey at Leestown became concrete. In 1857, Daniel Swigert invested in the future by creating a modest distillery at Leestown. There is no longer any doubt that the pedigree of the whiskeys of Buffalo Trace Distillery, in truth, began with Daniel Swigert in the late 1850s and not before.

The Kentucky River's Natural Wonders

As a major tributary of the Ohio River, the Kentucky River's watershed coverage area today comprises nearly 7,000 square miles of the Bluegrass, supplying fresh water to an estimated 17 percent of the commonwealth's north-central population, or about 700,000 people. A total of 14 locks were installed over several decades to control the river's erratic flow patterns. Lock no. 4 is situated at the city of Frankfort near the great buffalo trace. The only remaining navigable portion of the Kentucky River for sizeable craft starts at Lock no. 4 and spans all the way in a northwest direction to where its waters merge with those of the Ohio River at Carrolltown, Kentucky.

Doubtless, the most notable topographical feature of the Kentucky River, running from Clays Ferry to Frankfort, is the Kentucky River Palisades, the 100-mile long stretch in which steep gorges create breathtakingly photogenic backdrops. To ensure enjoyment for future generations, the Nature Conservancy protects the stunning and wild Palisades. The lofty walls of the limestone cliffs, some over 400 feet tall, provide homes and shelter for many species of birds, including peregrine falcons and kingfishers, as well as mammalian wildlife, such as bobcats, squirrels, and chipmunks.[a]

Yet, as idyllic as the Kentucky River is the majority of the time, when it overruns its banks due to backup from the Ohio River, it causes massive damage throughout much of its watershed area. In the records of the National Weather Service, an arm of the National Oceanic and Atmospheric Administration (NOAA), the Ohio River's top 10 flood events are led by "The Great Flood of 1937." Affecting an area from Pittsburgh, Pennsylvania, west to Louisville, Kentucky, and further downriver to Cairo, Illinois, a distance of 630 miles, the January 1937 inundation was so extreme that "geological evidence suggests that the 1937 flood outdid any previous flood."[b] The water lines are still visible at Buffalo Trace Distillery. Following the 1937 disaster the Army Corps of Engineers, under the direction of the U.S. Congress, improved the Kentucky River drainage through a massive program of channel clearances and the construction of levees and floodwalls. However, even in light of those structural improvements, more floods raged on the Kentucky River in March 1945, March 1964, and December 1978.[c]

More details on the Flood of 1937 and how it affected the Lees-town distilleries will come in a subsequent chapter.

Notes

a. Kentucky Unbridled Spirit: The Official Site of the Kentucky Department of Tourism.
b. National Weather Service, division of NOAA, "Top Ten Flood Events – Ohio River Valley."
c. Ibid.

5

"... The Machinery Is of the Best ... for Making Copper Distilled Whisky."

THE ONGOING DEBATE over the identity of Kentucky's initial whiskey distiller remains the catnip-like bait for some individuals with too much time on their hands. One hopes that at least the wheels of these pointless discussions are lubricated with tumblers filled with amber-colored bourbon. As to the identity of Kentucky's first distiller, names like Elijah Craig, Jacob Spears, Samuel Williams, Jacob Myers, James Pepper, Marsham Brashears, and Evan Williams are tossed about like WWE wrestlers and metal folding chairs at Wrestlemania.

The most reasonable settlement of this issue, in my view, is to acknowledge that whiskey distilling in north-central Kentucky materialized as something of a group consciousness effort by a small band of settler-distillers. They fired up their 5- to 20-gallon copper or log stills, circa 1775–1780, more to make full use of an excess of their corn harvest than to create fine bourbon. The distilling of whiskey was an afterthought, an agricultural practicality, rather than a top priority. Meticulous record or journal keeping by the frontier's widely dispersed communities likewise wasn't a higher matter of pre-eminence than the day-to-day survival tasks that included fetching clean water, feeding livestock, clearing fields, teaching the children to read, write, shoot rifles, and hunt, washing and mending clothes, baking bread, fixing fences, tilling fields, and cooking meals. Feckless personalities didn't thrive in the face of the brutality of the eighteenth-century wilderness. Until rock-hard evidence is brought forth, this debate will remain active solely for those who believe it is important. We should just all rejoice that the distilling of corn mash by primitive eighteenth-century distilling methods happened at all. An event that evolved into the industry we know and appreciate today.

With regard to the great buffalo trace location, the first incontestable evidence of formal distilling identifies Daniel Swigert in 1857 as being the owner of a compound on the Kentucky River that included the Leestown warehouse and more. In point of fact, in the autumn of 1858 Swigert put his riverfront compound up for sale. "FIRST RATE DISTILLERY FOR SALE," blares the headline of a print advertisement composed personally by Swigert in the October 8, 1858, edition of the *Western Citizen*, a Paris, Kentucky, periodical. Swigert's entire no-nonsense advertisement read as follows:

> Being about to engage in other pursuits, I offer for sale my Distillery and Fixtures. This property is about one mile below Frankfort, and just below the Lock, and within range of the proposed extensions of the water privileges. It has an excellent wharf perfectly convenient for the landing of coal, wood, grain, &c and equally so for the shipment of everything either up or down the river. The improvements consist of a large three-story stone warehouse, a still house, wood-house and excellent pens. The machinery is of the best and most approved patterns for making copper distilled Whisky. The engine is a splendid one and entirely new, having cost a few months hence, one thousand dollars. The establishment is supplied with a splendid spring of pure

water which never fails and never gets muddy. The property could, at a very trifling cost, be converted into one of the best and most eligible flouring mills in Kentucky. Anyone wishing to purchase will apply to me at my residence, adjacent to the premises.[1]

Oct. 8 D.	SWIGERT

Mister Swigert's "other pursuits," as it turned out, included most prominently the breeding of thoroughbred racehorses on his path to becoming an affluent Kentucky Bluegrass gentleman. A _New York Times_ story, titled "Spendthrift Farm Mob,"[2] that appeared in the May 6, 1978, edition confirmed Swigert's legacy as a noted breeder. Written by the legendary _Times_ sports columnist Red Smith, the article focused on memorable tales concerning the Kentucky Derby, including the creation of the highly successful Spendthrift Farm by Swigert's great-grandson, Leslie Combs, 2nd. Seeing as Daniel Swigert did not hanker to dirty his hands by being a distiller of Kentucky whiskey, there is speculation as to how much whiskey, if any, was produced in the fledgling riverside operation other than minute amounts needed to maintain the new equipment. It is reasonable to assume that the millhouse was operational to create flour. Yet, no record of actual whiskey production has yet been unearthed pertaining to Swigert's time of ownership. Daniel and Annette Swigert, in short order, sold the property on December 14, 1859, to Ashton and Clement Craig for the sum of $3,500.

". . . to lose Kentucky . . ."

The decade that followed the change of ownership of the Leestown property, the tumultuous period of 1860 to 1870, was impacted by the socioeconomic and political storm clouds that were stirred, first, by the American Civil War (1861–1865) and then by the gradual post-war recovery from 1865 to 1870. The war years were a tragically disruptive period for the state of Kentucky due to its precarious position as a so-called "border state." Because of its location between the northern tier of states and those of the south, Kentucky was neither fully Unionist nor Confederate. This positioning on the map caused Kentuckians significant angst as the tide of fighting rose in the autumn of 1861. Wrote Abraham Lincoln about Kentucky's vital situational importance in a September 22, 1861, letter to fellow Republican and Illinois Senator Orville H. Browning, "I think to lose Kentucky is nearly the same as to lose the whole game . . . Kentucky gone, we cannot hold Missouri, nor, as I think, Maryland. These all against us and the job on our hands is too large for us . . . We would as well consent to separation at once, including the surrender of this capitol."[3]

Both the Union and the Confederacy coveted Kentucky's allegiance as desperately as both wanted to command its strategic location. The key to its placement was having the critical Ohio River as its northern boundary. Even though the state's first official stance in 1861 as war broke out was one of neutrality, it eventually sided with the Union whose financial and commercial aid it needed to survive the ravages of the war. Though Kentucky's southern-leaning heart favored the cause of the Confederacy as evidenced by the fact that 25 percent of the state's 1860 population of 1,115,684 were slaves, its pragmatic head understood that cutting ties with the industrialized Union would potentially down the road cause grave economic injury, especially to its vibrant manufacturing sector that in 1860 was comprised of 3,450 companies. Those companies, representing more than $20,000,000 in invested capital, sold the overwhelming majority of their goods to the northern states and their cities prior to the war's first shots.[4] Losing the market that spanned from Illinois to Maine, Chicago to Boston would prove catastrophic in any postwar scenario. As a result, Kentucky, like Maryland, Delaware, and Missouri, the other "border states," suffered from the deep internal political divisions of its populace. The internal discord split communities and families between pro-Union abolitionist supporters and those favoring the Confederacy's staunch advocacy of the forcible ownership of human beings for the purpose of servitude, labor, profit, and subjugation.

Kentucky also served as a site for a series of battles, such as the pivotal blue-gray military engagements at the Battle of Richmond, fought on August 29 and 30 of 1862, and the fiercely contested and gory Battle of Perryville on October 8, 1862. The severity of the wartime activities and heated rhetoric strained the fabric of Kentucky society and proved to be a major hindrance for whiskey production, as scores of distilleries closed down or greatly curtailed production or, at the worst, were destroyed in the desperate actions of battle or retribution. With whiskey stocks flagging across Kentucky due to reduced production, whiskey became one of the most craved rarities across the country, both as a reward in difficult times for those who could afford it and medically as a reliable curative potion and hygienic liquid for those dealing with battlefield wounds and ailments. "In fact," reports the website for the American Battlefield Trust, "bourbon became so scarce that its price hit $40 per gallon in Richmond [Virginia], more than eight times that of bourbon sold in northern cities."[5]

In the vicinity of Leestown, Lexington, and Frankfort during the war years, Union soldiers' blue uniforms were commonly sighted as the troops of the north utilized the Kentucky River for the two-way movement of supplies, ammunition, cannon, and troops. In the summer of 1862, members of the Confederate cavalry took control of Frankfort and Lexington, as discussed in a telegram from the Confederate General John Hunt Morgan, in which Morgan claimed that his cavalry appeared to be ". . . sufficient to hold all the country outside Lexington and Frankfort. These places are garrisoned chiefly with Home Guards [local militia] . . ."[6] Morgan's occupation of the Bluegrass was short-lived and uneventful, though, due to his failed efforts to conscript young Kentucky men into the Confederate army. Other than those affairs and the depletion of hundreds of young, able-bodied men, the Bluegrass burghs escaped relatively unscathed the most damaging consequences of the conflict.

By early April 1865, it was clear to Kentuckians that the Union side led by the federal government under the steely stewardship of President Lincoln had vanquished the Confederacy and that it was time to repair the damage caused by four years of fighting and deprivation. Kentucky's whiskey makers were faced with the reality that in the aftermath of the war their corn-based bourbon had gained traction in the northern states as Union troops returned home to New England, New York, Pennsylvania,

Ohio, and New Jersey having sampled the quality of Kentucky whiskeys during their military service, tours that had them marching through border states as the fortunes of war shifted in favor of the Union forces. Consequently, Kentucky bourbon was suddenly competing with rye whiskey as the strong grain-based tipple of choice in the north.[7] It was incumbent upon Kentucky's distilling community by the late 1860s to gear up in order to meet the demand both from the eastern seaboard and the expanding communities in the western territories. Part of preparation meant modernizing and enlarging existing distilleries and building new ones. The profits were there for the taking.

Meanwhile, in Leestown, transactional activity concerning ownership of the Leestown distillery/warehouse property dated from the documented sale in 1859 to the Craigs up to 1870 is sketchy due purely to deficient Franklin County deed recordings and a paucity of regional newspaper reports. It is conceivable that this type of civil inefficiency or negligence was one of the instances of the type of collateral damage and bureaucratic disruption that came courtesy of the Civil War. Court records could also have been lost in the disastrous regional flood of 1937 that swamped both Leestown and Frankfort. Whatever the case, no data concerning the use of the distillery built by Daniel Swigert in the late 1850s by subsequent owners is available, even though familiar names linked with distilling like Blanton and Graham (of Labrot & Graham fame) were associated with the property. Since the Leestown landing site was utilized for the shipping of war materials during the Civil War period along the Kentucky River, it seems a stretch to conclude that regular schedule of distilling was possible.

But in November of 1870, a new era for Leestown distilling dawned when the dapper Colonel E. H. Taylor, Jr., an enterprising and charismatic banker from Lexington, purchased the property, lock, stock, shiny copper still, warehouse, and barrels, for $6,000 from Richard Tobin, James W. Graham, and S.I.M. Major. This change of ownership would propel the property at the great buffalo trace into the modern age of whiskey distilling and would serve to chart a thrilling new course for its history, one that impacts everyone who visits Buffalo Trace Distillery today.

Kentucky Whiskey Production: Grain

In order to make whiskey, any whiskey from anywhere, the distiller requires, as cited earlier, three easily attainable ingredients: grain, water, and yeast. In the late eighteenth century, a development – the rapid growth of agriculture – is well documented concerning the quartet of established District of Kentucky compounds, namely, Leestown, Harrodsburg, St. Asaph, and Boonesborough. In order to survive the wilderness, the cultivation of grains, in particular maize (corn), for the making of flour for bread, for the feeding of livestock and, eventually, for the distilling of grain alcohol from the grist became the most important consideration.

In his informative book, *Kentucky Bourbon: The Early Years of Whiskeymaking*, author Henry G. Crowgey observes, "The first grain crop was undeniably corn [maize], followed closely by small grain [wheat]; the first domestic fruits were apples and peaches. Richard Collins asserts that 'the first corn raised in Kentucky was in 1774, by John Harmon, in a field at the east end of Harrodsburg.'"[a] Crowgey's reference to Richard Collins comes from Collins's rewrite of the widely respected two-volume book, *History of Kentucky: Historical Sketches of Kentucky*, first authored by his father Lewis Collins.

There exist other reports of St. Asaph farmers growing corn in 1775 in fields covering more than 200 cleared acres. Nourished by the Bluegrass's fertile top soils and toasty, humid growing seasons, corn's remarkable productivity astonished the early settlers. Land speculator George Imlay in 1793 waxed poetically about corn's abundant yields in a report covering agriculture in the Bluegrass and Green River districts. Wrote Imlay, "Brandishing only fundamental tools, a newcomer could in the first year of settlement clear three acres of arable land, plant corn, and expect up to thirty bushels per acre. Playing this out further, just a single bushel of corn then provided enough seed to plant an additional twenty acres, which in turn could potentially provide a harvest of one thousand two hundred and fifty bushels."[b]

In an article written by Lewis H. Kilpatrick for *The Mississippi Valley Historical Review* in March of 1921 focusing on the journals of pioneer William Calk of Boonesborough, the matter of widespread corn cultivation in the frontier in the late 1770s is further cemented. In June of 1779, Calk and a friend John Harper constructed a log cabin ". . . described as being '14 feet long and 12 feet wide, well covered with sassafras puncheons' and floored with logs . . . It was about twenty to thirty poles southwest of the spring, fronting the buffalo trace. A clearing was made near by, fenced with rails, and planted in corn."[c]

Post–Civil War totals for statewide corn production in Kentucky skyrocketed, using the by-the-bushel metric. By 1890, Kentucky was responsible for producing roughly 78 million bushels of corn annually, with whiskey distillers using up 7.7 percent of the yearly harvest.[d] Kentucky's numerous municipal distilleries were especially anxious about securing enough bushels to fulfill their needs. One post–Civil War whiskey distillery located within Lexington's city limits begged for bushels of corn through a paid advertisement in the local newspaper, the *Lexington Observer and Reporter* in the autumn of 1867. The advertisement, titled, "Corn Wanted," read: "Farmers will please understand, we are always in the market [for corn], and willing to pay the highest cash price. We also want a few thousand bushels of No. 1 Rye."[e]

Notes

a. Henry G. Crowgey. *Kentucky Bourbon: The Early Years of Whiskeymaking.* Lexington: The University Press of Kentucky, 2008, p. 25.
b. Karl Raitz. *Making Bourbon: A Geographical History of Distilling in Nineteenth Century Kentucky.* Lexington: University Press of Kentucky, 2020, p. 57.
c. Lewis H. Kilpatrick. *The Mississippi Valley Historical Review.* March 1921.
d. Raitz. *Making Bourbon,* p. 62.
e. Ibid.

6

"... Bourbon Production ... Was at Best Crude and Unreliable ..."

THE POST-CIVIL WAR gentry that formed the beating heart of Kentucky Bluegrass's nineteenth-century societal elite went by surnames that included Swigert, Ware, Crittenden, Hay, Bacon, Rankin, Johnson, Saffell, Speed, and Taylor. The bloodlines of these core families overlapped in multigenerational intersecting circles, creating cousin-filled houses inside of patriarchal fiefdoms and distinct clans within the various familial dynasties. Together, the interconnected households shared business endeavors, traditionalist political viewpoints, fortunes, land holdings, top-level education, draped sitting rooms called *parlors*, and a joint line of descent that spanned generations. This ancestral dominion wrapped across the western and northern counties of the Commonwealth. Its heritage would be best chronicled by a spider-web-like flowchart, one with colored lines representing individual group clusters rather than by the typical multi-limbed genealogical tree. This privileged genealogical group was as much a business network as a lineage.

The existing sepia-tinted photographs paint elegant portraits of afflu-ence, fashion, and the gentility of a long bygone era. They are faded images of bearded gentlemen wearing top hats, smiling, robust children, and elegant women attired in lacey gowns. One can imagine that the conversations that drifted through the dominion's grand homes and manicured lawns in the last third of the 1800s were well-rehearsed exer-cises in cultured politeness, informed opinion, and conservative state and national politics, all served up in hushed tones and gentlemanly pats on the back. Often, these intimate conversations, bursting with ideas, plans of action, and theories, led to events that affected not only the lives of the blueblood clans but likewise of the Bluegrass citizens, the city of Frank-fort, and, on occasion, the entire state of Kentucky.

This was the world of influence and advantage that Edmund Haynes Taylor, the bright baby boy of Rebecca Edrington Taylor and John Eastin Taylor, was born into on February 12, 1830 in the western Kentucky sector known as Jackson Purchase. Young Edmund Haynes was a blood relation of two U.S. presidents, James Madison, the fourth president and a distant cousin, and Zachary Taylor, the 12th president and his great-uncle. Four of Edmund's relatives in the Taylor bloodline shared significant early connec-tions to Leestown, including two Taylors, Edmund and Reuben, who had accompanied British journalist Nicholas Cresswell in his expeditions of the Kentucky River in 1774–1775. The third was Commodore Richard Taylor, brother of Reuben and Edmund, whose initial visit to Kentucky from Vir-ginia was in the autumn of 1794. Over the ensuing years, the Commodore built himself a fine stone house that still stands near the Kentucky River within the Buffalo Trace Distillery campus. Richard's cousin was the slain surveyor Hancock Taylor. So, with Taylor family blood spilt on the riverbank sand of Leestown and Taylor observations and ambitions integrated into the charting of the locale, one can conclude with assurance that Edmund Haynes Taylor's boyhood impressions would have been animated with the folklore concerning the plot of land that lay near the great buffalo trace.

Yet in spite of Edmund Haynes's fortunate birthright, tragedy pierced his protective bubble in 1835 when his father, John Eastin Taylor, died of typhus at the age of 32. Reportedly, Taylor contracted the disease while returning to Kentucky from New Orleans. Typhus was a high mortality ailment that plagued many southerners of the era. The victim developed the malady once bitten by infected lice, fleas, ticks or mites. Due to his father's unexpected demise and according to the customs of the times, five-year-old Edmund Haynes, his sister Eugenia, and his mother Rebecca decamped from western Kentucky and moved to stately New Orleans to reside with their accommodating relative and the future U.S. president Zachary Taylor. In 1835, Taylor was serving as a colonel in the U.S. Army. Colonel Taylor's orders included supervising the erection of military barracks, safeguarding the newly built U.S. mint, and, in general, protecting the nation's interests along the wide expanse of the Mississippi River and its easily breached delta.

To his credit, Zachary Taylor made certain that his related young male charge received a solid education at Boyer's French School.[1] While in his teen years, Edmund returned to Kentucky in the late 1840s to live with his uncle and to complete his education at B.B. Sayre School in Frankfort. The elder Taylor was a prominent banker who coincidentally also was named Edmund Haynes Taylor. For the express purpose of clarification and to avoid public confusion, young Edmund added the "Junior" to his name even though technically he was not a junior. With his schooling soon behind him and in order to learn about the world of finances and commerce, E.H., Jr., at 19 years of age, took a position working in his uncle's prosperous Lexington bank, spearheading the opening of three branches.

In 1852 at the age of 22, E.H., Jr. became smitten with Frances Miller Johnson, a local young woman whose beauty was renowned throughout the Bluegrass. Frances, a member of the wealthy Johnson family, was called "Fanny" by her friends and by E.H., Jr. They married on December 21, 1852, and went on to have seven Taylor children: Jacob Swigert, Mary Belle, Rebecca, Kenner, Margaret Johnson, Edmund Watson, and Frances Allen.

By the late 1850s, the murmurings of conflict between the northern states and those south of the Mason-Dixon Line had developed into rage-filled shouts and vitriolic threats as the southern states debated breaking away from the Union. The disruptive news emanating out of Washington,

D.C., the capital of the United States, and Richmond, Virginia, the first city of the Confederacy, after the election of Abraham Lincoln as president in 1860 roiled the financial and commodities markets, adversely affecting investors and businessmen alike. After his marriage to Fanny, E.H., Jr. joined the private banking firm of Taylor, Turner & Company in 1854 as a partner. In 1855, the company became Taylor, Shelby & Company. But even Kentucky's banking community was not immune to the economic upheaval brought on by the national political turbulence. Upon the failure of Taylor, Shelby & Company, E.H., Jr. turned his attention to the business of commodities, a bustling and safe trade in the largely agricultural South.

War erupted in South Carolina in the spring of 1861 with the firing of Confederate cannon at Union-held Fort Sumter. E.H., Jr., like many of the Bluegrass hierarchy, favored the cause of the agrarian Confederacy, the custody of slaves for manual labor, and the ideals of its president Jefferson Davis. Taylor avoided military service for either side. Perhaps this happened through his well-oiled family connections, but that is pure conjecture. E.H., Jr., a man of renowned ambition and energy, remained in business throughout the war, profiting handsomely both from loaning money to the state of Kentucky, which was formally a Union-supporter, and by acting as an envoy to the cotton and tobacco growers of Tennessee. By the conclusion of the Civil War in early April of 1865, Fanny and E.H., Jr. found themselves sitting atop a veritable mountain of cash.

Following a months-long journey in 1866 throughout Europe, including tours of distilleries in France, Germany, Ireland, and Scotland, E.H., Jr. returned to Frankfort inspired by the Europeans' compelling distilling artistry.[2] His opening foray into the Kentucky whiskey business was as an investor in the Gaines, Berry & Company firm. Under the auspices of that company, E.H., Jr. participated in the supervision of the construction in 1867–1868 of The Hermitage Distillery, situated on the Kentucky River south of Frankfort. He also served in a financial advisory role for the Old Oscar Pepper Distillery on behalf of the teenage James Pepper, who had inherited "OOPD" from his father in 1864. Indeed, Taylor became James Pepper's legal guardian. The bourbons of OOPD, Old Pepper, and Old

Crow were viewed as among the finest of the day due in large measure to the technical prowess and scientific innovations of its fabled master distiller, the Scotsman Dr. James Crow (1789–1856).

The fact that OOPD bourbons were so acclaimed was not lost upon the inquisitive and perceptive mind of E.H., Jr. Thus by the late 1860s when the property at Leestown that included the three-story stone warehouse, the house called Stoney Point, a pure water spring, and a small distillery building nestled on 25 acres came on the market, E.H., Jr. was financially and experientially prepared to assume a more personal interest in the whiskey distilling industry. The enthralling yarns he had heard as a little boy of the frontier enclave known as Leestown and of the daring adventures of his cousins Richard, Reuben, Edmund, and Hancock Taylor now came full circle. On November 12, 1870, E.H. Taylor, Jr. signed the real estate contract that made him and Fanny the sole owners of Leestown, the choice riverfront property once coincidentally owned, if briefly, by Fanny's stepbrother-in-law, Daniel Swigert.

The Building of O.F.C.

Having experienced the business end of the distilling industry through The Hermitage Distillery in Frankfort and Old Oscar Pepper Distillery in nearby Woodford County, coupled with the data he gathered while on his European sojourn regarding the use of copper in the processes of fermentation and distillation, E.H., Jr. unleashed progressive and costly plans to upgrade and enlarge the existing Leestown Distillery, also known as Swigert's Old Distillery. After months of deliberation, he decided by early 1872 to demolish the three-story stone warehouse that had served as Swigert's modest distillery and build a new edifice for his wood-fired copper stills. His bottom-to-top design included installing copper fermentation tanks, 40-foot-tall copper column stills, state-of-the-art grain milling equipment, a modern and efficient system for making sour mash, and a revolutionary steam heating network for his warehouse to control the environmental air temperature during the maturation process. These innovative types of operating procedures were unheard of in whiskey circles in the early

1870s, where the most copper one might see in any Kentucky distillery involved a small, corroded orange-colored pot still tucked away in the hillside hamlets.

E.H., Jr.'s deep admiration for utilizing copper throughout the whole production process of whiskey-making inspired him to name his distillery at Leestown, O.F.C. The company's print advertisements highlighted its broad use of copper, claiming O.F.C. was ". . . the only distillery where the product is in contact with copper alone from the time the grain is ground until the finished whiskey is barreled in the splendid oak packages made at the company's cooper shops from selected and seasoned timber."[3] The construction cost to E.H., Jr. and Fanny was estimated to be between $60,000 and $70,000, more than a tidy sum for the period, even for a family of means.

Regarding the distillery name O.F.C., there are credible people, including family members, who insist that E.H., Jr. named his distillery Old *Fired* Copper while other reputable sources declare the given name to be Old *Fashioned* Copper. This debate has bedeviled archivists and historians alike for a century and a half. I, for one, spent parts of several weeks searching for a corroborated, clear-cut solution, reaching out to archivists, whiskey historians, and Buffalo Trace Distillery itself only to arrive at no conclusive answer, save that both versions have been and are still employed with abandon. After learning enough about E.H. Taylor, Jr. to gauge how his mind worked, my betting money lies more in the *Old Fired Copper* camp. It just seems to embody more of his flair for descriptive wording than the other middling version.

For all the moniker kerfuffle, one fact remains indisputable and iron-clad: the sour-mash bourbon whiskey made by E.H., Jr.'s production team at O.F.C. was from the start unlike any other whiskey at the time and considered by seasoned drinkers as better than all other whiskeys made in Kentucky. "Bourbon production in the Franklin County area was at best crude and unreliable until after the American Civil War. It was at this time that Colonel Edmund H. Taylor, Jr. is credited with revolutionizing the distilling industry within central Kentucky," wrote author Carl Kramer in his book, *Capital on the Kentucky: A Two Hundred Year History of Frankfort & Franklin County*.[4]

Colonel E.H. Taylor, Jr.

While the new technologies utilized at O.F.C. without question brought plenty of positive attention from the consuming public, E.H., Jr. himself placed great emphasis on his distilleries' water source as a major contributor to the quality of his whiskeys. The location near the great buffalo trace benefited from the pure spring waters that filtered through ancient limestone shelves, the Lower Silurian formations. A publicity booklet produced by E.H., Jr.'s company extolled the findings of geologist John H. Proctor, who created a *Map of Kentucky*, saying, "The O.F.C. and other brands of the E.H. Taylor, Jr. Co., are produced upon the depressed apex of this stratum, thus securing the best limestone drainage it can possibly afford. The result in fine whiskey is no doubt due to the water that, percolating through the limestone, becomes impregnated with its properties, and imparts them to the spirit during the process of manufacture ..."[5]

Later on in the booklet, a noted Louisville chemist, a Professor Barnum, is quoted as saying, "The water is of wonderful purity, and of peculiar adaptedness for the manufacture of whiskey."[6] The result of E.H., Jr.'s distilling success came in the form of demanding higher prices. Taylor sold his O.F.C. whiskeys by the gallon at roughly 20 cents more than any competitor.[7]

Clearly, O.F.C.'s groundbreaking methodology that included the use of small mash tubs and copper pot stills as well as copper column stills helped to transform the way that bourbon whiskey could be produced in the late nineteenth century and beyond. To that end, in fact, some of E.H., Jr.'s contemporaries were likewise committed to making more palatable whiskey through modernization and creative promotional thinking. George Garvin Brown, for instance, who would go on to create Brown-Forman, shook the whiskey industry of Kentucky to its core when he presented his Old Forester Bourbon in 1870, selling it only in bottles rather than by the barrel as a method to ensure consistent quality and authenticity. Talk about visionary. And Frederick Stitzel, another true whiskey pioneer originally from Alsace, brought long-term change to the whiskey industry of America when he was granted patent No. 9,175 on his unique modular system of racking barrels in his aging warehouses. Stitzel's ingenious four-wooden-post design allowed breathing space between the horizontally laid barrels and heralded a new era for the safe stacking of barrels. This was likewise the era that launched the concept of whiskey brands and the advertising and marketing that promoted them. It was as though having been released from the psychological and economic shackles imposed by the Civil War, Kentucky's whiskey distillers, as a group, intrepidly pressed forward to innovate and thereby blaze new trails.

But E.H., Jr. had the magic touch among his peers in terms of obtaining media attention and glowing newspaper stories. Reported Frankfort's *The Tri-Weekly Yeoman* on November 17, 1870, "The necessarily limited supply of this grade of fine whiskey [O.F.C.], and its conceded superiority, always commands for it a ready sale and liberal price. This fact, coupled with Mr. Taylor's reputation as a dealer, his experience and intelligence as a manufacturer, and his sagacity and energy as a businessman, will insure him complete success in this new enterprise."[8] Taylor himself couldn't have composed more flattering copy about O.F.C.

Yet, the distilling of noteworthy whiskey was only one element of E.H., Jr.'s chockfull life story. As a man blessed with a dazzling array of talents and pursuits, E.H., Jr. served as mayor of Frankfort for two terms, totaling 16 years, was elected as a state representative for Franklin County, and finally was a state senator of Kentucky's 20th district. In light of these admirable endeavors, however, one can't help but consider the premise that perhaps as his numerous interests and responsibilities mounted, they contributed, at least in part, to the deep financial troubles that would beset the O.F.C. Distillery a mere six years after it opened. And, further, his ambitions may be why he and Fanny were forced to place their model distillery at Leestown up for auction in 1878. Had E. H., Jr. taken his eye off the target through his pursuit of other interests?

Whatever the reasons, the historical record shows that a no-nonsense, button-down businessman, a retired Union army captain and a war hero from St. Louis, soon appeared to make his own imprint on the iconic whiskey distillery that the Taylors had built. His name was George T. Stagg.

7

"... That in Consideration of Five Hundred Dollars ..."

THE BUOYANT OUTLOOK of the post–Civil War years soon plummeted into an abyss caused by the global economic woes brought about by the Panic of 1873. The Panic's vice-like grip was felt all the way from the Ottoman Empire throughout Europe and the British Isles to the shores of North America for four apocalyptic years. Banks, stock markets, large and small businesses, municipalities, and entire industries crashed like meteorites into the sea. Preceded by the Great Chicago Fire of 1871 and the Great Boston Fire of 1872, the years 1873 to 1877 were dubbed "The Great Depression" by American newspaper wags, a full half-century before the twentieth century's own doomful version kicked off in October 1929. Recent history depicts with crystal clarity how the twentieth-century crisis led to world conflict, despair, and to depths of poverty never experienced before. The nineteenth century's Great Depression was set in motion by a parade of unfortunate socioeconomic and political events that began with the collapse of the Vienna stock market in May of 1873.[1] Anxiety spread like an August prairie fire and soon thereafter both France and Germany were gripped by recession. Great Britain's economy followed its Continental neighbors by falling into fiscal plight within weeks.

The United States fell prey in September of 1873 due in part to the ill effects of its own financial growing pains. First came President Ulysses S. Grant's demonetization of silver in favor of the gold standard through the Coinage Act of April 1873. This legislation swiftly devalued any of the cash money held in silver. Unfortunately, a sizeable percentage of money held by the nation's citizenry, banks, and small businesses was still in silver coins. Grant backed the controversial Coinage Act because by the 1870s the trend in U.S. currency was toward the use of paper or bank notes in commercial transactions. He was also reportedly influenced by Germany's monetary switch to the gold standard in July 1873. Silver coins were viewed as being the legal tender of an antiquated monetary system.[2] Grant's long-term vision was correct, but the short-term ramifications fed the beast of the looming Panic of 1873.

Then, the unanticipated collapse of the nation's most prominent bank, Jay Cooke & Company, after it badly miscalculated by overinvesting in the creation of railroads sent earthquake-like shocks through the domestic economy. Added to those woes was a crippling strike by railroad workers that shut down most commercial enterprises and the critical state-to-state chain of supply for goods, livestock, and food. The financial situation in the United States became so dire that the New York Stock Exchange closed for 10 straight days.[3] Political finger-pointing reached new lows as Republicans fought tooth and nail to maintain their fragile majorities in state legislatures and governors' mansions across the country. The Democrats, equally vitriolic, smelled blood in the water and acted with unbridled aggression. As a result, the U.S. Treasury foundered as it neared the state of collapse. Tempers, hysteria, and bombastic rhetoric ran high nationwide.

In Kentucky, the scene was as bleak as in any other region, characterized by fear, desperation, and cracks in the foundation of the financial system. Banks, businesses, and investors took severe beatings, including the

Taylor family. Loan money for first and second mortgages dried up. Lines of credit were summarily refused or dismissed. Inflation soared. Foreclosures mushroomed from state to state as loans were called in by lenders. People, the poor and middle classes especially, forfeited their homes, livelihoods, and their small and medium-sized businesses. The state's whiskey distillers suffered significant losses from meager revenues and the high cost of distillery maintenance and operation. These crippling trials were responsible for a substantial measure of the troubles that hounded the Taylors and their distillery, as their debt soared.

Yet, the bitterly cold wind gusts of worldwide and national stagnation weren't the only contributing factors to influence E.H., Jr. and Fanny's decision to place their beloved O.F.C. plant up for auction so they could pay their long list of creditors, a roster that included the Frankfort city Marshall, banks, a slew of local investors and friends, and even a minister.[4] During the same period, there was the surprising issue of E.H., Jr.'s inexplicably reckless handling of their business finances after the establishment of the distillery. During a period of economic recoil, Taylor's insatiable need to affect distillery improvements, most of which were financed on the flimsy platform of credit, was destined to implode. But that could be viewed as the best of Taylor's otherwise cavalier decisions.

Another unfathomable incident, in particular, from the period of 1875–1878 ended up in court, specifically the case of *Newcomb-Buchanan Co. v. Baskett*. The litigation came about when a short time prior to the 1877 Kentucky Derby E.H., Jr. sold 150 barrels of bourbon to a farmer from Henry County, J.S. Baskett, who shared a deep affinity with Taylor for Kentucky bourbon. Baskett reportedly yearned to have a visible presence in the whiskey industry. After Baskett dutifully kept his side of the transaction by paying Taylor in full for the bourbon, as well as the taxes, the whiskey, now legally the property of Baskett, was transferred to a free warehouse from Taylor's bonded warehouse at O.F.C. All on the up-and-up, right? Well, not quite. In order to cover his own debts, a portion of which were owed to George T. Stagg's firm, Gregory & Stagg, E.H., Jr. then turned around and sold the same 150 barrels to a distillery group, called Newcomb-Buchanan. Meanwhile, Newcomb-Buchanan, who were unaware of E.H., Jr.'s double-dealing, disposed of 25 barrels of Baskett's bourbon, presumably through a sale to a third party, and moved another 101 barrels to St. Louis to the premises of Gregory & Stagg to satisfy a portion of the debt owed by Taylor to Gregory & Stagg.[5]

When the unsuspecting J.S. Baskett went searching for his barrels during the summer of 1877, a mere 14 remained in the free warehouse. Worse, when he went looking for E.H., Jr. for an explanation he was told by associates that Taylor had quietly skipped town for parts unknown. To no one's surprise, that then instigated J.S. Baskett's lawsuit against Newcomb-Buchanan, which Baskett won, and which caused untold embarrassment to the proud Taylor clan. To where did Taylor flee? His great-great-grandson believes, as recorded in the Buffalo Trace Oral History Project,[6] that E.H., Jr., who is often referred to as a "bourbon aristocrat" or a "bourbon baron," bolted to Europe. He supposedly left one of his offspring behind to deal with the scandal. Court records from the lawsuit make the claim that, "In May, 1877, Taylor left the state on account of pecuniary [monetary] troubles . . ." Later in November of 1877, Taylor was asked by a reporter from the *Louisville Courier-Journal* about the episode,[7] "One more question, sir . . . How did you become embarrassed? That is to say, what causes operated to bring about your troubles?" To which Taylor responded, "Those which affected most everybody. I invested much in fine improvements. My O.F.C. distillery was considered the finest in the world. I tried to make it better than any in the land, and its reputation, all know, has never been equaled for pure, copper whisky. Sales stopped, money became tight, and before I knew it, interest exceeded earnings." Then the *Courier-Journal* reporter properly followed up by asking, "Why did you leave Frankfort?" Rationalized Taylor, "My presence would have done no good. Absence afforded an opportunity for thought and consultation."[8] Not to mention short-term escape from an awkward situation that was self-inflicted.

Because he eventually would satisfy his debts with the assistance of George T. Stagg and likewise due to his respected standing in the Kentucky whiskey industry, Taylor was able to ride out and eventually survive this onerous spell. Even his former adversary, the *Louisville Courier-Journal* in time became a vocal supporter, saying, ". . . the people of Frankfort are sincerely desirous of seeing Mr. Taylor effect an agreeable settlement with his creditors and to again engage in business."[9]

His contemporaries and allies would explain that E.H. Taylor, Jr. approached the distilling business with a banker's mind set of organizing an attractive plan, paying for it, then putting his vested interest up for sale to new investors to recoup his initial outlay and to make a profit. This is, in part, why Taylor was involved with seven distilleries over the course his lifetime. Unfortunately, throughout the troubled 1870s, Taylor's aspirations outweighed his financial reality, causing him to plunge into an ocean of red ink. His penchant for always having to produce the best possible product, as noble as this approach may have been, could not have been underwritten in view of the restraints of his monetary limitations. The cost of purchasing the finest equipment or of employing the most cutting-edge expertise proved to be higher than his ability to stay profitable. In the end, Taylor's greatest talents as a planner and an idea man who could make those intentions brick-and-mortar reality did not serve him well as a marketer of his goods as O.F.C. sales and revenues flagged. Therefore, E.H., Jr.'s decision to hire Gregory & Stagg to get his acclaimed whiskeys to the marketplace was an astute move but it came too late. By 1878, E.H., Jr. was drowning under the crushing weight of at the minimum $485,000 of unpaid bills, loans, and IOUs. He had no recourse but to declare bankruptcy and appeal to George T. Stagg to assist him by taking control of his valuable distillery property. Stagg, a calculating, dispassionate observer, saw opportunity in Taylor's misfortune. Once his control was solidified through the transfer of ownership, Stagg restructured the company finances and paid off the laundry list of creditors, redeeming to some degree Taylor's reputation.

Realizing the continuing profitability and potential of O.F.C., Stagg and Gregory decided to keep the crown jewel distillery active. "To pay off his indebtedness to Stagg and his partner Clay Gregory, Taylor the next year had to sign over his distillery properties, including the O.F.C. distillery," writes Taylor family descendent Richard Taylor in his book *The Great Crossing*.[10] The transfer agreement between E.H. Taylor, Jr., his wife Fanny Taylor, and George T. Stagg, as recorded in Franklin County Deed Book 16, page 51 on March 22, 1879, reads in part, ". . . That in consideration of Five Hundred dollars in hand paid the receipt of which is hereby acknowledged the parties of the first part [the Taylors] sell, convey and confirm unto the party of the second part [G.T. Stagg] and his heirs and assigns the following described lot or parcel of land situated in Franklin County Kentucky on the Kentucky river . . ."

Compelled by the desire to help smooth the transition as well as to ensure a measure of continuity for the whiskey brand, E.H., Jr. at Stagg's urging agreed to stay on as a company director and vice president of operations, overseeing all whiskey production. Taylor and Stagg, as different as chalk and cheese in personality and business outlook, one a riot of brilliant colors and the other subtle shades of gray, clashed on a regular basis. It didn't help that according to the company's original restructuring upon the close of the deal, Stagg's share in the company amounted to 3,448 shares while E.H., Jr.'s was a measly 1 share.[11] The vexatious Taylor-Stagg relationship lasted for over six years. In 1879, Stagg reorganized the company, rechristening it as the E.H. Taylor, Jr. Company. As the majority stockholder, he made himself president. Stagg cunningly kept the Taylor name because he understood that as a producer of superior whiskey, Taylor's prominence and fame remained recognized far beyond the burghs of Frankfort, Lexington, and Louisville. Taylor's name could only help to promote the brand. The firm title, however, would cause further friction between them in the future.

With whiskey sales accelerating once again in the late 1870s with the economy recovering from the Panic of 1873, Stagg and Taylor built the Carlisle Distillery, along with a string of warehouses directly to the north of O.F.C. on the old Leestown riverbank site. Carlisle's function, however, was markedly different from O.F.C.'s much ballyhooed "handmade" tradition. Its operation was on a more industrial scale for the purpose of creating sizeable volumes of grain spirit. For instance, while O.F.C.'s promotional materials highlighted its use of small mash tubs that were stirred by hand, Carlisle was fitted with large machine-driven mash tubs. There was no "hands-on" approach with Carlisle. O.F.C. and Carlisle would end up being big volume producers. Production capacity, with full governmental approval, for each distillery was from 40 to 50 barrels of whiskey per day from 500 bushels of grain. For the time, those were substantial numbers.

A correspondent to the Louisville Courier-Journal described with precision the operations of O.F.C. and Carlisle, writing, ". . . They [O.F.C.

and Carlisle] consist of two sour mash distilleries, six immense bonded warehouses . . .Their aggregate capacity is 60,000 barrels, one which holds 20,000 and another 10,500 barrels. Three of these warehouses are supplied with patent ricks, and all are iron-clad and fireproof and provided with covered gutters to carry off any liquor to the river in case of accident . . . The two distilleries are large and ornate buildings, brick and stone, three stories high, one 260 by 60 feet, the other 220 by 60 feet, each complete in every detail from the splendid complement of engines down to the array of hundreds of mash tubs, flake stands and fermenters, all under cover and protected from wind and weather . . . In the manufacture of the O.F.C. brand all the old traditions of the early distillers are strictly observed and carried out to the letter. The famous old distillers, such as Crow and others of his period, became renowned for the purity of water and materials used and for adhering faithfully and honestly, under all circumstances, to the simple hand-made process."[12]

To expand the holdings and production capability of what was legally then George T. Stagg's whiskey company, a third modest-sized distillery, the J. Swigert Taylor Distillery, located a half dozen miles from Frankfort in Woodford County, was purchased in 1882. It was operated by one of E.H., Jr.'s sons, Jacob Swigert Taylor. But with tensions irretrievably boiling over between Stagg and the older Taylor for over a half dozen years, E.H., Jr.'s tenure with the company named after him eventually came to an unpleasant end. In October 1885, Stagg accepted Taylor's resignation. Much of the next year, 1886, was consumed with wrangling over the division of assets of the E.H. Taylor, Jr. Company. The final binding agreement stipulated that Stagg give Taylor and his sons the small-scale J. Swigert Taylor Distillery in exchange for the relinquishing of all of Taylor's interests in E.H. Taylor, Jr. Company. Stagg even agreed, by some accounts through a verbal but not written guarantee, to remove Taylor's name from the company, though he later changed his mind and retained it.

The separation was complete. Stagg, the man who bailed Taylor out of bankruptcy to rescue O.F.C., and the Taylor family were at last rid of each other. Temporarily. Regrettably as we shall shortly see, the men would again confront each other in the coming years due to a series of lawsuits filed by Taylor against Stagg.

After departing E.H. Taylor, Jr. Company for good, Taylor, together with his sons Jacob Swigert Taylor and Kenner Taylor, established a new firm, E.H. Taylor & Sons. Within months, they plotted the future course for their Woodford County distillery, which they renamed Old Taylor Distillery. The property was a 136-acre parcel situated close to the Old Crow Distillery. By the end of the nineteenth century, Old Taylor Distillery on Glenn's Creek was recognized as being an even grander showplace than O.F.C. The Old Taylor distillery building itself resembled a medieval castle. Visitors upon entering were treated to a *gratis* "tenth pint" of Old Taylor and were encouraged to stay for a picnic on the landscaped grounds. Everything about Old Taylor was imbued with E.H. Jr.'s natural gift for marketing and promotion, including the whiskey, which was widely praised. Sales were brisk.

But Taylor's status as a whiskey business elder in his later years would become even more storied for his eloquent and persistent public defense of the quality and authenticity of Kentucky whiskey. This recognition was spawned by his pivotal and passionate role in the fight for the passing of the groundbreaking Bottled-in-Bond Act.

8

"Rev. Dr. McLeod Thanks God for Duffy's Pure Malt Whiskey"

THE CONCEPT OF "consumer protection," so prevalent nowadays through the guiding edicts provided through both state and federal lawmakers and agencies, was not a hot-button topic in the second half of the nineteenth century. Rather, in the middle of the 1800s, duping the public about the authenticity of what they were imbibing or eating was considered to be fair game. Otherwise, why would an unabashed charlatan and opportunist named Pierre Lacour have the temerity to publish and sell a book called *The Manufacture of Liquors, Wines and Cordials Without the Art of Distillation* in 1853?[1] In short, what Lacour was overtly touting with impunity was the unregulated mimicking of authentic, hand-made distillates, most prominently, whiskey, by recklessly mixing straight ethanol with other dubious compounds. These compounds included turpentine, beets, oak bark, wintergreen, tobacco, iodine, prune juice, and more all for the purpose of creating a sham product that to the eye of the unsuspecting buyer may have resembled real whiskey, remotely smelled and tasted marginally like whiskey, but was made at a fraction of the cost, expertise, and time of the genuine article. Most critically, these widely available counterfeit liquids were not whiskey by any definition. Many, in fact, were dangerous to consume.

The post–Civil War period from 1865 to 1900 was rife with every conceivable type of snake oil salesman and con artist. One huckster of particular note from Rochester, New York, however, stands out as much for his audacity as for his success. Walter B. Duffy (1840–1911) was the producer of perhaps the era's most infamous phony whiskey and cure-all, Duffy's Pure Malt Whiskey.[2] With a straight face, Duffy made the outrageous claims that Duffy's Pure Malt when used medicinally could help you outlive your children, could cure cancer, influenza, indigestion, gout, and bronchitis. Without a doubt, his most infamous claim and my personal favorite was that Duffy's could cure ugliness. I ponder the possibilities of that wild claim just within my family alone.

Duffy's print advertisements unabashedly ran the slogan "Makes The Weak Strong," alongside pictures of clergymen and nurses endorsing the bogus elixir. "Rev. Dr. McLeod Thanks God for Duffy's Pure Malt Whiskey" read one preposterous advertisement. Another screamed in a large typesize, "GRIP, CONSUMPTION CURED." In their best light, such claims and practices were outrageous fakery, pure and simple. When hoax whiskey brands with evocative names like Old Roanoke, Old Bourbon, and Monangahela began flooding the U.S. marketplace, competing with and, in the process, undercutting the bona fide whiskeys offered by legitimate distillers, the domestic whiskey industry was outraged.[3] To brandish this type of chicanery as an activity of merit and profit was a sucker punch in the face to those scores of distillers around the nation who took pride in their craft and what they lawfully offered to the public.

In Kentucky, where whiskey distilling had advanced to the same elite status as that of the state's other source of intense pride, thoroughbred racehorse breeding, the impostors' activities were heatedly discussed in the clubs and taverns where the Bluegrass distillers convened. One particular voice of indignation, when heard, would quiet the room. It was the voice of the E.H. Taylor, Jr. Among Taylor's primary concerns, he told his peers, was that the products made by the fraudsters would place doubt in the minds of the drinking public, whose uncertainty concerning product authenticity might then taint their views of all whiskeys being offered, including Kentucky's fine bourbons. That was unacceptable. Taylor argued that war had to be declared on these unscrupulous quacks by persuading the federal government to become involved, most preferably as a guarantor of provenance and legitimacy. Kentucky's whiskey producers rallied around the articulate Taylor.

So in 1893, Taylor and other Kentucky whiskey men began pleading their case in Washington, D.C., at hearings in the halls of Congress. With Secretary of the Treasury John G. Carlisle as a key ally, the distillers embarked on a tedious four-year odyssey of vigorous debate and petition with members of Congress. Then on March 3, 1897, the 54th United States Congress enacted the Bottled-in-Bond Act,[4] rewarding the Kentucky whiskey distillers' united efforts for the cause of veracity and integrity. The landmark legislation gave distillers the green light to bottle their spirits straight from their bonded warehouses under government agent supervision.

The strict guidelines of the Bottled-in-Bond Act, officially codified as Title 27 CFR 5.42,[5] as they still apply today, are as follows:

1. Spirits are distilled in the same distilling season, either January to June or July to December.
2. All distillation happens at one distillery only.
3. Spirits are matured for at least four years in wooden containers in a federally bonded warehouse that is under federal official supervision.
4. Spirits are bottled at 100-proof, or 50 percent alcohol by volume.
5. The distillery of origin is clearly identified on the label.
6. Label identifies the bottling location, if different than the distillery or distiller.
7. Nothing other than water is added to reduce the proof to 100.

Once these guidelines had been met, the product was permitted to receive a green stamp that was attached to the bottle, certifying the authenticity of the bottle's contents. Today, the green stamp certifications are infrequently used, leaving the authenticity verification to the usage of the wording on the label. The legislation of Title 27 CFR 5.42(b) (3) specifies that the words "bond," "bottled-in-bond," or "used-in-bond" can appear on the label and are considered sufficient validations. Also, the Act allows for any type of matured distillate to be bottled-in-bond, not just whiskey. There currently are a handful of American brandies, including Laird's Straight Apple Brandy and Christian Brothers Sacred Bond, that are bottled under these guidelines.

Historically speaking, the passage of this bill heralded the dawn of consumer protection from the illegal practices of scam artists and unethical producers of all types of consumable product industries, not just whiskey. This milestone legislation evolved into a precursor that led to other pivotal acts of consumer protection later in the opening decades of the twentieth century. These included the 1906 Pure Food and Drug Act, the 1906 Federal Meat Inspection Act, the 1938 Food, Drug and Cosmetic Act, and others. No minor achievement, this.

In the final analysis of this episode, two results are crystal clear. First, the Bottled-in-Bond Act represented a major victory across the commercial board for the cause of genuineness, public safety, and commercial honesty and accountability. It kicked off the national discussion of how government can play an active role in the protection of the governed. Second, the leadership and resolve displayed by E.H. Taylor, Jr. from the very start of the action through the responsible declaration by Congress secured his place as a revered champion in the cause of Kentucky whiskey-making by preserving its authenticity.

While E.H. Taylor, Jr., like any one of us, had character flaws and peccadilloes, few early Kentucky distillers achieved the list of accomplishments and renown that he had. Taylor, who died in Frankfort on January 19, 1923, in the early days of Prohibition at the age of 92, had the innate gift of envisioning what could be and, moreover, then knew how to make it happen. Even in view of his financial misjudgments, E.H. Taylor, Jr.'s larger legacy of being a dedicated whiskey man lives on. Inspired by a combination of grand ideas, production genius, sense of style, and progressive thinking, his indelible mark remains an industry standard to the present day.

In a fitting tribute, since 2011 Buffalo Trace Distillery has honored Taylor's memory and legacy by offering a line of straight ryes and bourbons under his name, Col. E.H. Taylor, Jr. All expressions, with the exception of the few barrel-strength bottlings, are Bottled-in-Bond whiskeys at the legal 50 percent alcohol by volume level. The "colonel" indication, to be clear, is not a military-related moniker, but rather is an honor bestowed ceremoniously to Kentuckians of illustrious endeavors.

In the end, even George T. Stagg would have had to agree that E.H. Taylor, Jr. deserved and earned the accolade of "bourbon aristocrat."

9

"The Most Valuable Assistance That We Got in St. Louis . . ."

PRIOR TO BECOMING a respected whiskey agent in St. Louis, Missouri, and later the owner of the celebrated O.F.C. and Carlisle distilleries in Frankfort, Kentucky, George Thomas Stagg was a Union officer who served with valor for the entire four-year span of the U.S. Civil War. A fervent opponent of slavery, he enlisted into the Union Army in Kentucky in November of 1861.[1] Steely and strong, Stagg quickly gained the reputation of being a skilled bare-knuckle pugilist. Through a field commission Stagg rose to 1st Lieutenant status in January of 1862. One year later, Stagg was elevated to the rank of Captain in the D and I Companies of the 21st Kentucky Infantry in the aftermath of a furious battle fought at Stones River. In 1863, he was selected to be General Ambrose Burnside's aide-de-camp. With every promotion, Stagg exhibited his commendable organizational abilities, his unwavering loyalty to his regiment and commanding officers, and his unmatched leadership skills.[2] George Thomas Stagg, in other words, proved under fire to be a model soldier and leader.

The Union Army's 21st Kentucky Infantry (KI) was no ordinary regiment. It was a disciplined, proficient fighting machine. The warriors of the 21st KI engaged in numerous critical confrontations, often involving brutally desperate hand-to-hand combat, featuring knives, rifle butts, fists, and bayonets that dripped with blood and severed flesh.[3] Stagg and his men made heroic battlefield charges racing headlong into the blistering fire of Confederate rifles and artillery. Throughout Kentucky, Tennessee, Alabama, and Georgia, the 21st routed, killed, and captured hundreds of Rebel forces. Their most fateful encounters included the Battles of Franklin, of Nashville, of Stones River, and of Kennesaw Mountain. They also participated in the siege of Atlanta at the conclusion of the war. Upon finishing their term of service in the city of New Orleans in June of 1865, Union Brigadier General Jefferson C. Davis lavished praise on the 21st KI, saying, ". . . no regiment exhibited a higher state of discipline and efficiency in the whole [Union] army than the Twenty-First Kentucky Infantry."[4]

But, in Stagg's mind, all the praise and pomp would never resurrect the 200-plus soldiers and fellow officers of the 21st KI regiment who perished either in the heat of mortal combat or, just as tragically, to the diseases that ran rampant on the battlefields. True to his character, Stagg stoically endured and ended his military career with dignity and little fanfare. He returned to Kentucky not a diminished man, but instead a canny, observant, and resolute hero. The lessons Stagg learned on the battlefield concerning selfless bravery under the severest fire and of remaining calm and steadfast in unimaginably chaotic circumstances were emblazoned on his psyche for the rest of his life, both in professional and private affairs. Stagg's honorable service in the Civil War paid homage to his great-grandfather James Stagg, who fought in the Revolutionary War as a Regimental Commander with the New Jersey Militia. Service to country and to the ideals of freedom and equality for all citizens were inherent in the Stagg family.

Born in December of 1835 in Garrard County, Kentucky, George T. Stagg grew up in a strict and orderly household. His parents were guided

George Thomas Stagg

by the tenets of his European ancestors, who had been members of the Dutch Reformed Church in the Netherlands. In 1858 at the age of 23, Stagg married Elizabeth "Bettie" Doolin, settling with her in Richmond, Kentucky to raise a family. Before entering his army service in the Civil War, Stagg was employed as a clerk in a shore store.

Returning from four years of military service, Stagg and Bettie relocated from central Kentucky to the bustling city of St. Louis. Brimming with opportunity, St. Louis was booming mostly from its strategic location as a major hub of commercial river traffic. With city boundaries expanding and an industrious population of over 200,000, St. Louis was the perfect urban fit for the Staggs. George's serious demeanor, solid family background, and sterling war record made finding a suitable employment position a sure bet. Following an interview with James Gregory, a wealthy Missouri businessman who was evidently impressed by the 31-year-old Stagg, a new company was formed, Gregory & Stagg, Commercial Merchants & Distillers' Agents.[5]

In 1875, the upstanding Stagg became a primary whistle-blower in a booze-related scandal, the so-called "Whiskey Ring." Stagg caught wind of distillers, rectifiers, storekeepers, and their governmental accomplices, a band of compromised federal tax agents, defrauding the U.S. government in order to evade paying taxes on whiskey production. The damning evidence unearthed by investigators eventually led all the way to President Ulysses S. Grant's personal secretary, Orville Babcock. Though no allegations were issued directly implicating Grant, the matter stained his presidency.

The criminal activity involved illegal whiskey getting dumped in a St. Louis warehouse before being surreptitiously transported to the port of New Orleans. Stagg proved to be a key witness in the ensuing investigation. After lawyers for the defense accused Stagg as being complicit, Elverton R. Chapman, a federal Internal Revenue officer, defended him, saying, "The most valuable assistance that we got in St. Louis was from George T. Stagg, of the firm of Gregory & Stagg, commission-merchants in St. Louis. Mr. Stagg is entitled to more credit for the exposure of the St. Louis whiskey ring than any other man that lives."[6] In the end, the special prosecutor John Brooks Henderson, who had been personally appointed by the Republican President Ulysses S. Grant, recovered more than $3 million in stolen tax money and won 110 convictions.

Taylor and Stagg: Born to Disagree

Gregory & Stagg acted as distributors and go-betweens for the whiskey distillers of Kentucky and the nation's marketplaces. Stagg's sober and polite personality made inroads immediately with urban and rural merchants who bought whiskey by the barrel and then sold it throughout the Midwest. His contact list of the genuine distillers and rectifiers in the American heartland became a major source of profit for Gregory & Stagg. One of those names on Stagg's list was the charismatic and well-spoken Kentucky colonel who was considered by industry observers to be the headlining whiskey distiller of the period, E.H. Taylor, Jr., proprietor of the hallowed O.F.C. Distillery. Stagg's visits to the distillery in Frankfort built upon the old Leestown site would, as we have already seen, in part turn into a critically important chapter of the Buffalo Trace story.

Following his contentious breakup with E.H. Taylor, Jr. in 1885, Stagg was forced to spend a greater amount of time in Frankfort, Kentucky than at his family home in St. Louis. Stagg quickly realized that the successful supervision of a large distillery operation required the on-site presence of a decisive production manager more than the owner. Control and the adherence to protocols were paramount to Stagg. With his military service and Gregory & Stagg careers being accentuated by his keen sense of responsibility and full commitment, Stagg felt compelled to devote most of his time at the distillery to ensure that the stellar reputation of O.F.C. remained untainted.

After a fire caused by a lightning strike had destroyed most of the O.F.C. plant years earlier in June of 1882, Stagg's nemesis and partner at the time, E.H. Taylor, Jr., oversaw the rebuilding project in 1883. The new O.F.C., as devised by Taylor, was even grander and more modern than the old distillery, which was saying a lot. In a brochure about the O.F.C. and Carlisle distilleries and warehouses created by the media-conscious Taylor just before his resignation in late 1885, detailed illustrations showed the buildings' positions in relation to the Kentucky River and the Leestown landing at the great buffalo trace.

The continued success of the new George T. Stagg Company that now owned O.F.C. and Carlisle was buoyed entirely on the products of the distilleries. This reality weighed heavily on George T. Stagg during the post-Taylor years as his expertise was in sales, not whiskey production. After his split with Taylor, Stagg closed both O.F.C. and Carlisle for a year and a half to upgrade much of the equipment. Production resumed at the plants in January of 1889. By all accounts, the whiskeys maintained their high degree of quality after the plant reopened. Then, trouble began brewing once again between the two bitter adversaries. Acknowledging that the name "Taylor" held a particular resonance with whiskey lovers around the nation, Stagg decided to reinstate that reputable name for the company title to boost sales. It may have seemed like a sound business choice to Stagg in the solace of his office at O.F.C., but publicly his reversal looked to be an avoidable misstep. Thus, what had been the George T. Stagg Company after the breakup of Stagg and Taylor reverted back to the E.H. Taylor, Jr. Company.

Upon hearing of Stagg's decision to bring back the company name of E.H. Taylor, Jr. Company without consent or consultation from the namesake, Taylor was infuriated. This unilateral action by Stagg triggered a series of costly and time-consuming lawsuits brought by Taylor against Stagg and his partners that wound their way through various levels of courts for a decade. Perhaps the most famous individual legal action issued by Taylor concerned Stagg's right to use of Taylor's elaborate script signature as a marketing tool. On October 16, 1889, Taylor's lawyers requested that Stagg cease using the company name of E.H. Taylor, Jr. Company and that he no longer use Taylor's signature on barrels or in advertising.[7] An injunction to the stoppages was filed. The request also asked for damages in addition to the cessation of the employment of Taylor's name and signature. Since Taylor was no longer the distiller at O.F.C. and Carlisle, the court granted the injunction in Taylor's favor, but it did not award him damages. This partial victory did not satisfy Taylor, who requested that the court re-examine the ruling on the damages.

Undeterred by his court defeats, Taylor kept pursuing the damages. In 1896, the Kentucky Court of Appeals upheld the original ruling, not allowing the payment of damages.[8] Incensed even more, Taylor marched his legal crusade back into the lower courts, eventually winning damages from Stagg's company, perhaps due to the court's fatigue of the matter. Unflinching, Stagg's company countersued Taylor, bringing this over-ripe dispute once again before the Kentucky Court of Appeals in 1902, where the higher court ruled once again in the Stagg Company's favor, thereby striking down the damages ruling once and for all. Thirteen years of toxic legal bickering between Taylor and Stagg and his company ended at last.[9]

In the meantime, George T. Stagg retired in 1890 and died three years later in 1893 at the age of 57. The breakup of Taylor and Stagg affected Stagg, it now appears, more than Taylor. With Taylor's departure, Stagg was thinly stretched, running both the George T. Stagg Distillery in Frankfort and leading the sales force of Gregory & Stagg in St. Louis. As a witness in another U.S. Senate investigation that followed the Whiskey Ring action, Stagg described in his testimony how difficult his daily routine had become, saying, "I am scarcely in St. Louis. I have not been there, perhaps, for more than a few days at a time for a year and a half, or two years . . . I do selling for these houses in the Eastern markets."[10]

But, hold on, because this tale of the Frankfort distilleries in the late nineteenth century takes an even stranger twist in the years just prior to, and immediately after, Stagg's death. In the closing of what can only be described as a peculiar, if ironic, circle, Stagg, his health then flagging, retired in 1890 and returned to his family home in St. Louis. After Stagg's formal departure, the notorious flimflam distiller from Rochester, New York who was the mastermind behind Duffy's Pure Malt Whiskey, Walter P. Duffy, secretly gobbled up Stagg's sizeable stock holdings, making him the majority owner of the prestigious George T. Stagg Company. While Duffy's tenure as proprietor of O.F.C. and Carlisle was largely uneventful through the 1890s, it is hard to imagine that the straight-laced George T. Stagg ever approved of Duffy's takeover. One can only wonder if perhaps Stagg should have slammed back some of Duffy's Pure Malt Whiskey for what had ailed him. Yet, in terms of a lasting legacy, George T. Stagg's name now adorns a powerful, cask-strength, and unfiltered straight bourbon that is, in 2021, recognized as being one of Buffalo Trace Distillery's greatest treasures in its galaxy of American spirits.

In consideration of the complicated Taylor-Stagg relationship, it would be the height of understatement to claim that their fractious bond laid the foundation for the future triumphs at the George Stagg & Company distillery and through later incarnations to become Buffalo Trace. For although Taylor and Stagg fought tooth and nail over most business issues, their individual intentions and talents to make superior Kentucky bourbon whiskey operated on parallel tracks. Convincing them to agree on anything may have been as simple as teaching chickens to line dance, yet together, in spite of themselves, they made outstanding whiskeys for a handful of years at O.F.C. and Carlisle.

Later, when separated by mutual contempt, life directions, and legal actions, they each continued to excel at producing highly sought-after whiskeys, E.H. Taylor, Jr. at Old Taylor Distillery and George T. Stagg at O.F.C. Make no mistake that as the historical record confirms, the perpetuation of American whiskey production and quality excellence in the waning decades of the 1800s is their joint epitaph.

10

"...An Early Nineteenth Century Residence Situated in the Middle of an Expansive Lawn..."

E.H. Taylor, Jr. served as mayor of Frankfort for the second time from 1881 to 1890. By all accounts, it was a successful term. Frankfort, the community founded by the American Revolutionary War scoundrel James Wilkerson, was well positioned then to grow in the decade leading up to the turn of the century. Divided by the Kentucky River, it was a heartland city that in the 1890s buzzed with the promise of commercial success, civic advancements, and broad prosperity. Frankfort's population exploded from 3,702 in 1860 to 9,487 in 1900.[1] New mercantile businesses, banks (State National Bank), schools (The Clinton Street School), and hotels (Buhr Hotel) opened to serve the booming population and the vibrant traffic within the business districts. Flour mills, lumber mills, and

83

meat-packing plants all churned with the industrial clamor of labor, their wares transported via the local railway system, the Frankfort & Cincinnati Railroad, or by riverboat. No less than 12 distilleries were active in Frankfort in 1898, producing an impressive 600 barrels of whiskey daily.[2]

Near the close of the nineteenth century, the Leestown landing, first surveyed by the McAfees and settled by the Lees more than a century before, was bustling with commercial enterprise. The commotion at the crossing site caused earlier by the hooves of migrating buffalo, the passage of tribal hunting parties, and the idle chatter of wandering settlers was in 1890 generated by the noise of workmen employed by the O.F.C. Distillery that was renamed George T. Stagg Distillery in 1904[3] and the Kentucky River Mills, the hemp processing plant that was erected in 1877–1878. The Carlisle Distillery underwent a major renovation in the autumn of 1898 and was rechristened as the Kentucky River Distillery.[4] Together, the three facilities were the source of steady employment for scores of Frankfort residents, as well as tax revenues for the city coffers.

The chiming of streetcar bells could be heard echoing along the primary streets of Frankfort by 1894. One streetcar line operated on a track running from the heart of central Frankfort to the O.F.C. Distillery along Wilkerson Boulevard. From the second-floor room in his family home, known as The Beeches, young Albert Bacon Blanton perhaps could hear the clanging of the bells as the streetcars deliberately crept their way up and down the boulevard hill. Harrison Blanton, Albert's grandfather, built the initial parts of The Beeches on its Leestown site, circa 1810–1812. The property was described as follows in the nomination form for the National Registry of Historic Places Inventory: "The Beeches is an early nineteenth century residence situated in the middle of an expansive lawn immediately southeast of the Leestown Pike (U.S. 421) and within the corporate limits of Frankfort, Kentucky. This brick house combines a 1½-story section of an earlier residence with a 2½-story main block erected in 1818. Later brick and frame additions are at the rear and on the east. Across Leestown Pike (made four-lanes in recent years) are the brick warehouses of the Stagg Distillery Company."[5]

The Blanton family genealogy is an amalgamation of the Ware, the Bacon, the Combs, and the Blanton clans that all hailed from the eighteenth-century Virginia Colony. Albert, born on February 28, 1881, was the son of Benjamin Harrison Blanton (1829–1884) and Alice Elizabeth Bacon (1843–1917) of Philadelphia, Pennsylvania. Albert's father had been a prospector in California who struck gold in 1849. A passage from the book *A Sesqui-Centennial History of Kentucky* by Frederick A. Wallis and Hambleton Tapp noted, ". . . in the fifties he owned most of the business section of downtown Denver, Colorado, property which, in his enthusiasm for the Southern [Confederacy] cause, he exchanged for bonds of the Confederacy. These eventually became worthless. In the war between the States, Benjamin Harrison Blanton served as major on the staff of General Hood, surviving the battle of Gettysburg and other battles, without a scratch . . ."[6] After completing his military service, Benjamin Harrison Blanton returned to Frankfort, his boyhood home turf.

Albert's industrious grandfather Harrison Blanton (1791–1879) had settled in Kentucky with his family in 1799. The elder Blanton, who had close ties to the Leestown site, gained fame in the early 1800s as a builder of grand houses. From 1827 to 1830, he supplied the limestone for the Old State Capitol building. Taken from notes on the 1860 census, Harrison Blanton is identified as a farmer with $12,500 in land holdings and $6,000 on personal property.[7] Tidy sums at the time.

Clever, studious, and ambitious from an early age, Albert Bacon Blanton completed his Frankfort district schooling early. The O.F.C. Distillery hired Blanton in 1887 at the age of 16 in the position of office boy. On his own time, Albert learned shorthand and typing skills.[8] Proving to be a capable young man, Blanton ascended the employment ladder, switching from the office job to a post dealing with barrel management and racking on the warehouse staff. He was then promoted to the Receiving Department, but that assignment didn't last long as shortly thereafter he jumped to operating the gristmill. After four productive years, Albert Blanton finally landed onto the floor of the distilling room.

Blanton's natural skills, quick wittedness, and accelerating business acumen kept his opportunities unlimited. At the age of 31 to the surprise of no one, Blanton became the distillery superintendent, overseeing all functions of the warehouses, the bottling facility, and the distilling operations.[9] In 1921, after 34 years of loyal service, Albert Blanton assumed the

Albert Bacon Blanton

post of President of the George T. Stagg Distillery, completing a fixed and steady rise in the Kentucky whiskey industry.

But as easy as his career climb may have seemed early on, challenges lay ahead for Albert Blanton, monumental challenges brought on by external forces that were far beyond his control. At 12:01 a.m. on January 17, 1920, the Volstead Act, named after Minnesota Representative Andrew J. Volstead, compelled by the ratification of the 18th Amendment to the U.S. Constitution one year earlier, took effect. Enacted over Woodrow Wilson's presidential veto, the Volstead Act gave the federal government the set of legal tools it needed to enforce the prohibition of beverage alcohol throughout the entire nation. This legislation not only upended production in the Kentucky whiskey industry, permanently closing the majority of the Commonwealth's 180 distillers, but sent the domestic beverage industry, the nation's fifth largest business sector at the time, into a disastrous tailspin. In Louisville alone, for example, it is estimated that 6,000 to 8,000 jobs related to the distilling industry were lost. For 13 interminable years, the United States floundered socially and economically due to the grim quagmire known as the Prohibition Era.

How had Prohibition come about when so many citizens assumed that such a draconian measure would never become reality? In brief terms, the 18th Amendment was instigated in the first half of the 1800s by a powerful anti-alcohol coalition led by the temperance and suffragette movements, as well as political reform parties, like the National Prohibition Reform Party. Their collective actions were a powerful backlash to the amount of alcohol being consumed on a per capita basis in the early 1800s, an astounding seven gallons of pure alcohol annually. This figure in contemporary terms would mean that each adult was drinking almost two 750-milliliter bottles of 80-proof liquor every week. Or to view it another way, that's slightly more than 100 bottles for each adult, mostly men, per year, including the millions of citizens who were teetotalers. Fact is, with well over 14,000 distilleries active across the country by 1810, liquor was ubiquitous.[10] There is no question about the nineteenth-century reality that insobriety was widespread and was thus a primary cause of an epidemic of family strife.

The 18th Amendment declared "the production, transport, and sale of intoxicating liquors" to be illegal across the nation. The "intoxicating liquors" included any consumable liquid with alcohol in it, meaning, beer, wine, and distilled spirits such as whiskey. No state was spared from the wrath of "The Great Experiment," even whiskey-loving Kentucky. In fact, anti-alcohol parades and demonstrations were commonplace throughout Kentucky as early as the 1830s. Many of the Prohibition movement's chief firebrands, such as Carrie Nation, John Hickman, Frances Estill Beauchamp, and George Washington Bain, crisscrossed the state, speaking at rallies to whip up support and even invading bars and saloons to disturb the patrons. By 1907, 95 of Kentucky's 119 counties were considered "dry," meaning that by law, alcohol production and sales were forbidden. The well-funded and politically savvy anti-alcohol groups, such as the Women's Christian Temperance Union, Anti-Saloon League, and the Independent Order of Good Templars, scored a historic, if temporary, constitutional victory whose reverberations are still felt decades later. Even the racially radical Ku Klux Klan was considered an anti-alcohol advocate group.

"This brings me now to the dark days of National Prohibition," wrote Albert Blanton in the early 1950s. ". . . and they were dark days – nothing but confusion as I don't believe many ever realized that we were really going to have Prohibition, and we didn't have much for the first two years. I, for one, never thought it would last as long as it did."[11]

As events played out throughout the 1920s and early 1930s, Prohibition failed to effectively ban alcohol at all in the 48 states as ghost bars, popularly known as "speakeasies," mushroomed by the thousands in every metropolitan region and even in most out-of-the-way rural sectors. Underground nightclubs sprang up in Louisville and Lexington, to the consternation of local police forces. Black-market booze, like "bathtub gin," flowed like Niagara Falls. What the Volstead Act did end up accomplishing through Prohibition was the near-bankruptcy of the U.S. Treasury due to the termination of booze tax collection, estimated to be a loss of $11 billion.[12] That is not to mention the government expenditure of $300 million to enforce Prohibition. The Act also erased the jobs and financial security of thousands of distillery, brewery, trucking, and winery workers in addition to the thousands of hospitality industry workers and food suppliers whose jobs were lost. The Great Experiment also tilled the fertile ground out of which grew the monstrous creation of organized crime, spearheaded by Italian, Jewish, and Irish gangs, who ran the production, sale, and transportation of illicit liquor from New York to Los Angeles and from Mexico to Canada.

Strangely, while the wording in the Volstead Act didn't explicitly prohibit the consumption of alcoholic beverages, the banning of production shut down virtually all distilleries across the country except for a half-dozen distillers, of whom George T. Stagg was one. In addition to George T. Stagg, or Frankfort Distillers as it was also known, the other survivors of the liquor ban included Brown-Forman, Stitzel Distillery, James Thompson and Brother, Schenley Distilleries, and American Medicinal Spirits, which would later become the distilling giant, National Distillers, the brainchild of spirits baron Seton Porter.

To his great fortune, Albert Blanton was able to keep George T. Stagg Distillery's lights flickering and doors open under the banner of being a federally designated "concentration warehouse." This government-generated moniker afforded Blanton the license to store thousands of barrels of whiskey in the Stagg warehouses from other Kentucky distilleries that had been boarded up. How much whiskey was being warehoused one year before Prohibition? "In 1919, national Prohibition officials estimated that 50 million gallons of whiskey sat in bonded warehouses . . . The initial Prohibition legislation allowed for medicinal whiskey and sacramental wine . . ."[13] This tally of 50 million gallons had an approximated value of $400 million.

In a classic case of providing cold comfort, The Liquor Concentration Act of 1922 and the provision allowing alcohol production for medicinal purposes allowed Blanton to not only warehouse barreled whiskey of his own and other distillers but likewise to produce small amounts of whiskey at Stagg for the finest-tasting cough medicine ever made. Whiskey prescribed as medicine, you ask? Damn straight. Pharmacies flourished during Prohibition, legally selling medicinal whiskey by the pint. A big beneficiary, for instance, was Chicago-based Walgreens that went from owning 20 drug stores in 1919 to 397 stores in 1930. As late as the early twentieth century, societal norms and a slight majority of the medical profession and pharmacists still viewed potables, in particular brandy, rum, and whiskey, as curative and therapeutic elixirs that were worthy of being prescribed to their patients. Indeed, Kentucky was one of 26 states that sanctioned whiskey as a medicine by prescription all during Prohibition.

This liberal viewpoint of *hard liquor* may have been helped, in part, by the lightning-fast spread in 1918 of the cataclysmic Spanish flu pandemic that took the lives of an estimated 675,000 American citizens. One account from a medical eyewitness during the pandemic said, "According to navy nurse Josie Brown, who worked in the Navy Hospital in the Great Lakes in 1918, 'We would give them a little hot whiskey toddy; that's about all we had time to do.'"[14]

As president of George T. Stagg Company, Albert Blanton was just pleased to comply with the medicinal mandate in order to keep some of his distillery's equipment operational, at least until the lifting of Prohibition by the passing of the 21st Amendment. But in 1929, four years before the enactment of the Repeal of Prohibition, Blanton by his own personal account became concerned as the company's whiskey inventories began to run low. He had to have pondered, "What happens when Prohibition is lifted?"

"A moderate amount of bottling and shipping was done through the years until the Summer of 1929 when at that time owing to depletion of stocks of whiskey in bonded warehouses the need of replenishing for future needs became more and more apparent and my first thought was by all means to get this plant in operation again," recollected Blanton in his memoir.[15]

The owners of George T. Stagg at the time were the aforementioned Walter P. Duffy of Rochester, New York and Henry M. Naylon of Buffalo, New York. Upon hearing Blanton's reasonable concerns, the upstate New Yorkers balked, telling him that they did not have the interest in spending lots of capital to get the distilleries operational prior to the uncertain repeal of Prohibition. "With the one purpose that this plant must go on," wrote Blanton, "I persuaded Mr. Naylon that it would be best to dispose of the properties to someone who would be in the position to market the balance of the whiskey and resume operation of the distillery when the Government authorized the manufacture of additional stocks . . . He and all interests fully agreed that this was the best course to pursue, and it was not long before negotiations started with Mr. [Lewis] Rosenstiel and Sidney L. Hellman, his partner, with the result that Schenley Products Co. took over as of October, 1, 1929 . . ."[16]

If anything could be said about Albert Bacon Blanton, it was that he lived for the welfare of his beloved distillery and employees, so this transaction, engineered mostly by him, made complete sense. The new owners, Lewis Rosenstiel and Sidney L. Hellman, instantly recognized Blanton's devotion, integrity, and perspicacity and asked him to remain as operational manager. They would have been halfwits to think otherwise. As we shall see shortly, no one could or would ever accuse the street-smart Rosenstiel and Hellman of being fools. Blanton later reminisced, "I remained with the new ownership, and I feel that I did the former owners a real service when I helped engineer the sale to Schenley, and as have stated elsewhere, I have no regret whatever over the change in ownership and same has been profitable to me and mostly so to this community which is a great source of gratification to me."[17]

Build Thee an Ark, Albert

By the mid-1920s, it was clear to the American public and the majority of politicians that Prohibition's "Great Experiment" was a disaster at every level, socially, economically, politically, and with regard to public safety. State and national political sentiment was then being swayed by a growing number of anti-Prohibition groups, like the Women's Organization for National Prohibition Reform. The outcry in the nation's print media to repeal the 18th Amendment was reinforced by the stock market crash of October 1929. The economically struggling public grew weary of reading about how ruthless gangsters like Al Capone, Lucky Luciano, Meyer Lansky, Johnny Torrio, Bugsy Segal, Arnold Rothstein, and "Nucky" Johnson were illegally raking in millions of dollars by running bootleg operations, often under the protection of bribed local police forces, district attorneys, and even judges. With the U.S. economy in tatters, with corruption rampant, and with the Treasury in serious trouble of defaulting, the tide of public opinion against Prohibition swelled into a tsunami.

Given impetus by the election of Democrat Franklin Delano Roosevelt as the new president, Prohibition was repealed nationally in December of 1933 with the passing of the 21st Amendment. Kentucky, however, was slower out of the repeal gate, with the combative Governor Ruby Laffon, known by opponents as "the terrible Turk from Madisonville," not lifting all restrictions inexplicably until May 18, 1934. Under new ownership, the George T. Stagg Company guided by the calm captaincy of Albert Blanton geared up for full production capacity to meet the expected wave of whiskey sales from a parched public. As Blanton described in his own words, "In the Fall of 1933 with the repeal of the 18th Amendment in sight, every effort was made to increase production and by erecting additional fermenting tubs and adding other necessary equipment, including the old distilling apparatus from the Jas. E. Pepper & Co. distillery at Lexington, KY, the mashing capacity was stepped up to 1,514 bushels on October 9, 1933, and to 3,602 bushels on December 13, 1933, and all increases were made while the plant continued in operation."[18]

Backed by the full financial and industrial might of Schenley and the business savvy primarily of Lewis Rosenstiel, Blanton continued his relentless march for production expansion through the next few years as public demand for quality Kentucky whiskey snowballed. From 1934 onward, Blanton, to Rosenstiel's delight, had his distillery working at full capacity. In the spring of 1935, plans were drawn up for the building of a new, modern distillery plant. The pace was furious, as described by Blanton, "The work of building a milling department, mash house, fermenting house and yeast room, still house and cistern room together with additional warehouses was rushed during the summer without reducing production although one of the new buildings, the fermenting house, was built over and around a building housing a greater part of fermenters being used daily . . ."[19] With a fortuitous track line extension of the Frankfort & Cincinnati Railroad then running directly to the distillery complex, shipments of Old Stagg whiskey were being transported via truck and rail to all the key eastern and Midwestern markets.

One year earlier, in 1934, Albert Blanton married Vannie B. Stevens of Anderson County, Kentucky, and, with Lewis Rosenstiel's blessing, built a handsome residence, called Rock Hill on company property. Perched above the distillery compound, Rock Hill afforded Albert and Vannie a prime view of George T. Stagg Company, all the way to the Kentucky River. Following the nightmare of 13 years of disappointment brought about by Prohibition, times had turned brighter and more fulfilling, brimming with hope and optimism.

Then a little over three years after the repeal of Prohibition came January 6, 1937, a cloud-shrouded, angry hound of a Wednesday on which rains cascaded down in sheets from the gunmetal gray sky. And that was just the launching point of the unprecedented deluge that would soon eclipse all other previous recorded floods on the Kentucky River and across the Ohio River Valley as ". . . a chain of cataclysmic storms hovered over the central part of Kentucky and the Ohio Valley and produced . . . devastating record flood levels over three weeks."[20] The great precipitation spigot in the sky remained agape for 20 days as storm after storm inundated the huge area from southern Illinois in the west to the city of Pittsburgh, Pennsylvania in the east. An estimated 42 quadrillion gallons of water in all its climatological forms – rain, snow, sleet, and ice – filled the trough-like region of the Ohio River Valley in unrelenting squalls. Kentucky's historical average precipitation for the entire month of January is between a mere 3 to 4 inches. Across the 417-mile width of Kentucky in January of 1937 the average precipitation was 15.77 inches, with many areas receiving up to 24 inches, amounts for which the state was unprepared.

The Ohio River raged for days at 34 feet *above* flood stage for 981 miles, meaning that all the mighty river's tributaries, including the Kentucky River, were swamped upstream. The Ohio's highest point was a head-spinning 75.3 feet at Maysville, Kentucky. More than two million residents had to be evacuated from northern Kentucky, southern Ohio, southern Illinois, southwestern Pennsylvania, and southern Indiana. Immersed highways and railways prevented travel between isolated Kentucky communities. Electric power was shut down in most of the commonwealth. Martial law had to be declared in several towns and cities, including Louisville, to maintain order, to assist emergency services, and to prevent looting.

In Frankfort, more than half of the city's neighborhoods, both affluent and downtrodden alike, were submerged by January 27. The affected areas included, of course, the low-lying, riverside George T. Stagg distilling complex, as the normally placid Kentucky River crested at an unimaginable height of 47.2 feet. Nearly all the plant's facilities and buildings, including Warehouse H, which housed Albert Blanton's favorite bourbons, were at the minimum under four feet of frigid, brown, and turgid river water. Though the Flood of '37 was a disaster for Kentucky on a biblical scale, Albert Blanton never evacuated the company compound. Deciding instead to ride out the period with a few hearty and trusted distillery workers, Blanton defied the floodwaters while trying to protect as much of the valuable distillery machinery and equipment and whiskey inventory as possible. Based on the fact that George T. Stagg Distillery was reportedly up and operational within two days of the conclusion of the torrential rains while neighboring plants took months to recover, it appears that Blanton's daring decision to ride out the storms paid off.[21] Albert Blanton's steely nerve, decisiveness, and determined leadership under the duress of the severest of natural disasters was not lost upon those who watched, most importantly Lewis Rosenstiel, from the recently relocated Schenley headquarters situated in the six-year-old Empire State Building in midtown Manhattan.

11

"...Raised the Daily Production from 400 to 600 Barrels..."

PRIOR TO SCHENLEY'S purchase of the George T. Stagg Company in 1929, the seeds that sprouted Schenley Products were originally sown in Armstrong County, Pennsylvania in the form of the Schenley Distillery. Lewis Rosenstiel was but one year old when the distillery opened in 1892. Later, in 1918, at the age of 26, Lewis Rosenstiel's connection to whiskey took a fateful turn when he became the superintendent of the Susquemac Distillery, owned by his uncle, David L. Johnson. That job regrettably ended with the closure of the plant at the start of Prohibition.[1]

With the financial assistance of the investment-banking firm Lehman Brothers, Rosenstiel and a group of like-minded associates next opened the Cincinnati Distributing Corporation in Cincinnati, Ohio, a concern that sold bulk medicinal whiskey. One of those associates was Sidney L. Hellman, who would later command Schenley Products Company alongside Rosenstiel. Believing that he and Hellman needed to prepare for the eventual repeal of Prohibition, Rosenstiel purchased in 1920 the Joseph S. Finch Distillery for the sole purpose of acquiring its half-million gallons of Golden Wedding Whiskey. Thrown in with the deal was something else of considerable value: the plant's whiskey concentration permit issued by the U.S. government.[2]

While on vacation on the French Riviera in the summer of 1922, Rosenstiel encountered Winston Churchill, who at that time was a parliamentary member of Britain's Liberal Party. Churchill, according to the New York Times obituary of Lewis Rosenstiel, ". . . advised him [Rosenstiel] to prepare for the return of liquor sales in the United States."[3] Heeding Churchill's counsel, Rosenstiel returned home more confident in his beliefs and wasted no time in acquiring more key distillery properties, such as the Schenley Distillery in 1923 with its 4,000 barrels of mature whiskey and four aging warehouses. In his one-pointed pursuit of amassing more whiskey reserves, Rosenstiel then bought 240,000 cases of Old Overholt Rye Whiskey in 1927, which at that time was the single biggest purchase of aged whiskey during the Prohibition years.[4]

But even these sizeable reserves weren't enough in Rosenstiel's view because in his mind once Prohibition was lifted, the stir-crazy nation would go berserk buying and drinking quality, properly aged whiskey. Thirteen seemingly endless years of the consumption of "rotgut," the foul-tasting, fake whiskeys, rums, brandies, and gins produced frequently by unscrupulous, unskilled amateurs would certainly trigger a stampede to vendors and distilleries that offered the genuine articles. Lewis Rosenstiel, by his own admission, understood the fragility of human nature and its inherent need to satisfy its greedy bank of senses. Among his many attributes, Rosenstiel was a master at the art of acute observation and character analysis. Based on these calculated abilities, he would in time create a beverage alcohol empire.

In the wake of the stock market crash of 1929, Rosenstiel and his cronies accelerated their acquisition efforts. Between 1929 and 1933, Rosenstiel's Schenley Products Company signed the deals that brought into their fold the prime distilleries of George T. Stagg of Frankfort, Kentucky, James E. Pepper of Lexington, Kentucky, and Old Quaker of

Lawrenceburg, Indiana, to be known later as Midwest Grain Products (MGP) Distillery.

For his unwavering service, Albert Blanton was made a vice president of Schenley Products Company and remained as the plant manager at George T. Stagg. In July of 1933 in anticipation of Prohibition's repeal, the Schenley Products Company became Schenley Distillers Corporation with the filing of papers by Schenley attorneys in the state of Delaware. To no one's surprise, Rosenstiel was listed as chairman. Harold Jacobi was identified as president. The Schenley Distillers Corporation was to serve as the protective corporate umbrella, beneath which no less than 15 companies operated throughout the Ohio River Valley, distilling, storing, and shipping whiskey and other spirits while employing thousands of workers.[5]

By the time that the 21st Amendment was being ratified on the state-by-state level in the middle of 1933, Rosenstiel and his corporation owned a staggering array of ready-to-sell matured whiskey, including the popular brands of Old Stagg, Golden Wedding, Gibson, Monticello, James E. Pepper, Sam Thompson, Silver Wedding, Greenbrier, and Schenley. Thus, on the cusp of the repeal of the 18th Amendment by the passage of the 21st Amendment by the Congress of the United States in late 1933, Schenley Distillers Corporation stood poised to supply a country of legal-age spirits drinkers with hundreds of thousands of gallons of matured-in-barrel whiskey.

Meanwhile back in Frankfort, Thanksgiving of 1933 had come and gone. Albert Blanton knew that once the state of Utah became the 36th state to ratify the 21st Amendment on December 5, 1933, thereby providing the three-fourths majority of states required for passage, that he would be expected by Lewis Rosenstiel to immediately bring the George T. Stagg whiskey distilleries back up to full speed. After all, Rosenstiel reminded Blanton, the thirsty nation, deprived of joy, would soon be calling. And in startling numbers, Americans did. By the middle of 1934, sales boomed for Rosenstiel's company. By the year's end, Schenley had earned $6.9 million net on gross sales of $40.3 million; for the day, a massive sum. The next year, 1935, gross sales of $63 million netted $8 million.[6] Schenley's flagship whiskeys were flying off shelves across the nation. The top brands

1933 aerial photograph of George T. Stagg Distillery campus

of Old Stagg, Cream of Kentucky, Old Quaker, Jas. E. Pepper, Golden
Wedding, and Old Schenley, in particular, could be found on thousands of
backbars and retail shelves in establishments from New York to Chicago
to Denver to San Francisco.

From 1934 on, Albert Blanton's distillery teams were working double shifts in Kentucky and Indiana to meet the avalanche of demand for
Old Stagg, Old Schenley Reserve, Three Feathers Reserve, Three Feathers V.S.R., Old Quaker, and Cream of Kentucky straight and bottled-in-
bond whiskeys. Just a few weeks after the Flood of 1937, an April 12,
1937, article headline in the *Lexington Herald-Leader* read, "Stagg Output
Is Stepped Up Substantially." Reported the article, "An increase of fifty
percent in the daily production of whiskey at the Geo. T. Stagg Company
plant followed another increase of ten percent was recently announced
by Col. A. B. Blanton, plant manager. The increase, which raised the

daily production from 400 to 600 barrels, then from 600 to 660, consumes another 2,600 bushels of grain each day and resulted in the promotion of many company employees and employment of a similar number of new employees, Colonel Blanton said."[7]

To bolster its place as a leading North American beverage company second only to Samuel Bronfman's Montreal-based juggernaut Joseph E. Seagram & Sons, purchased by Bronfman in 1928, Schenley also held exclusive distribution rights starting in the mid- to late 1930s to top European spirits brands, such as Otard Cognac, Dubonnet, Cherry Herring, and Dewar's White Label Blended Scotch Whisky. In 1936, the company introduced the Ancient Age whiskey brand. The company also began importing and distributing Bacardi Rum in 1938. Rosenstiel and his team proved to be voracious, smart, and calculating in their acquisitions.

As the years rolled on past the 1930s and into the early 1940s, Lewis Rosenstiel kept adding more responsibilities to his main man in Kentucky, Albert Blanton. Almost a victim of his own reliability and organizational brilliance, in addition to remaining the lord of the manor at George T. Stagg, Blanton also took on the roles of leading the James E. Pepper Distilling Company, the Schenley Distilleries Company at Stamping Ground, the Blue Ribbon Distilleries Company of Carrollton, and the Schenley Distilleries at Burgin. Though all the facilities were located in Kentucky, Blanton's managerial duties had to be enormously taxing. For his decades of loyal service, Blanton was also made a corporate vice president and a member of the board of Schenley Industries, Inc. In addition to these responsibilities, he was a respected member of the Kentucky Distillers Association.

Just before the United States entered World War II in late 1941 after the Japanese attacked Pearl Harbor, Rosenstiel ordered Blanton and his chief maintenance engineer at Stagg, Orville Schupp, to prepare the company's group of distilleries for the mass production of high-proof alcohol through the construction of special column stills.[8] Rosenstiel envisioned the coming need for cheap, easily produced high-proof alcohol for the looming war effort for a raft of things, such as antifreeze for military vehicles, plastics, synthetic rubber, lacquer, rayon for parachutes, and antiseptics. In the end, the U.S. government requested America's distilleries to produce 50,000,000 gallons of industrial alcohol. The power of Schenley Industries also contributed to the production of penicillin, a much-needed wartime medical need.

From early 1942 through 1945, Rosenstiel's plants were working three eight-hour shifts seven day a week. During the global conflict, the disruption to Schenley's workforce was significant, as many younger staff members, mostly males, went off to serve either in the European or Pacific battle theaters. As a sign of Rosenstiel's need to placate the labor unions and to demonstrate company loyalty, the family of any serviceman or service woman was guaranteed to receive a portion of the employee's salary each month in which they served. Plus servicemen were promised to have their company position waiting for them upon their return from combat. In the meantime, to meet the demand for workers, Schenley first hired African-Americans and then women to fill the roles left open by the departing servicemen.

Astonishingly, even beneath the burden of the distillery's war effort duties, in 1942, Blanton, his newly named plant superintendent, Orville Schupp, and their crew celebrated the production of the millionth barrel of whiskey that was produced at George T. Stagg following Prohibition. The next year, Blanton curtailed a measure of his daily activities, handing off some of the Stagg plant operations and other distillery commitments to the able Schupp. After being employed at George T. Stagg for 55 years with a robust record of achievement, Blanton retired in 1952. Predictably, Blanton was succeeded by his talented protégé, Orville Schupp, who himself had been grooming a bright young plant worker since 1949 by the name of Elmer T. Lee.

Albert Blanton's death seven years later in 1959 at the age of 78 plunged the whiskey industry into a state of mourning. Beloved by friends and competitors alike for his courtly and courteous demeanor, Albert Bacon Blanton embodied the ideal of the Kentucky Colonel, the nonmilitary honor bestowed upon a celebrated few. As the dean of American distillers in his twilight years, Blanton never lost his sense of humility or his sense of gratitude for a life well lived. The plaque inscription on the statute of Blanton that was erected within the Buffalo Trace complex reads:

Loved and Respected

Master Distillers And

True Kentucky Gentleman.

He Dedicated 55 Years Of His

Life To The Service Of

His Community And His Company.

That His Inspired Leadership

May Live In The Minds Of Those

With Whom He Lived And Of

Those Who Follow. This Memorial

Is Erected With Gratitude And Honor.

In the November 1952 edition of the company newspaper, the *Schenley News*, Lewis Rosenstiel's testimonial to his long-time employee Albert Blanton, titled, "Tribute to Col. Albert B. Blanton on the occasion of retirement dinner . . . At Geo. T. Stagg clubhouse, Frankfort, Kentucky, November 14, 1952" was printed. In the tribute, Rosenstiel's admiration after more than 27 years of friendship is evident. After reading it, one has to believe that it must have been a powerful moment to experience in person. Said Rosenstiel in part, "I have come here tonight to pay homage and respect to a great man, a true friend, and one who has been an inspiration to me . . . Albert is the very essence of kindness to everyone – even his enemies; he may be blunt, and sometimes, though rarely, I have seen him quite angry; but he has never been unkind and he has never for an instant lost that fine spirit of reserve, which is so truly wonderful . . . He has always been Mr. Kentucky to me, a bluegrass gentlemen in every sense of the word."[9]

At the conclusion of his tribute, Rosenstiel announced to Albert and Vannie Blanton that he had put forth a resolution to the Schenley board of directors that the George T. Stagg Distillery would be renamed the

Albert B. Blanton Distillery. The resolution passed by a unanimous vote. But while the distillery name was officially changed, it was still referred to within the industry either as the George T. Stagg Distillery or the Leestown Distillery until it became Buffalo Trace Distillery in 1999.

As were the footprints left by his predecessors E.H. Taylor, Jr. and George T. Stagg, Albert Blanton's legacy as one of the most esteemed Kentucky whiskey men indelibly linked to the Leestown distilleries would be commemorated in the coming decades by one of his successors, master distiller Elmer T. Lee. And Lee's liquid memorial to Blanton would, unbeknownst to Lee, usher in the second Golden Age of Bourbon.

12

"Despite Many Salacious Rumors, He Is Mostly Remembered As . . ."

AFTER THE DEEPLY troubled first half of the twentieth century that included the horrors of World War I, Prohibition, the Great Depression, and World War II, the decade of the 1950s featured a relatively upbeat period of optimism and industrial recovery in the United States for some sectors of society. To be sure, the Korean War in the early 1950s caused hardship for those who served, as well as geopolitical concerns, but by 1955 the American populace was eagerly looking to the future. The nation still had long strides to make on numerous social and racial issues, mainly civil rights, women's rights, equitable voting rights, just immigration laws, and more accessible education opportunities.

But, many Americans were feeling the bounce from the victory in World War II as they, for the most part, imbibed two classic distillates: whiskey and gin. From straight bourbons and ryes, American and

Canadian blended whiskeys, to whiskey-based cocktails such as highballs, whiskey sours, whiskey and sodas, and whiskey and ginger ales, the bar was OPEN in all 48 states. The mild and gently sweet blended whiskeys, especially category-leading Seagram 7 Crown and Seagram VO Canadian Whisky brands, skyrocketed in popularity. These affordable spirits were user-friendly marriages of convenience that combined small amounts (20 to 25 percent) of full-bodied straight whiskey with larger percentages (75–80 percent) of ethereal neutral grain spirit that was, for all intents and purposes, vodka. These two ubiquitous brands in particular sold in the hundreds of thousands of cases annually during the 1950s. Print ads for Seagram 7 Crown in 1950 promised, "ALL ROADS LEAD TO AMERICA'S FAVORITE 7 . . . Say Seagram's And Be Sure." And, "From here to the golden gate. . .it is the first and foremost whiskey in the land – Say Seagram's And Be Sure." The Seagram blended whiskeys lined the coffers of Joseph E. Seagram & Sons with a steady torrent of profits from the late 1940s to the mid-1970s, as they traded the number-one and number-two spots as the best-selling spirits brands during these years.

Schenley's own versions of blended whiskey were Schenley Black Label, which was made up of 67 percent neutral grain spirits and 33 percent straight whiskey, and Schenley Red Label, comprised of a whopping 72.5 percent neutral grain spirits and 27.5 percent straight whiskey. The straight whiskey portion was divided between 17.5 percent four-year-old and 10 percent five-year-old whiskey.[1] While they sold well in some markets, Schenley's case sales were never in the same league as Seagram's dynamic duo. This reportedly always irked the competitive Lewis Rosenstiel, who always strove to best his archrival Samuel Bronfman, the CEO of Joseph E. Seagram.

Due to their deep stocks, the roster of whiskeys offered by Schenley in the 1950s was long and varied, with many brands offering multiple distinctive expressions at different proofs and ages. This avalanche of brands served the purpose of dominating retail shelves in all U.S. markets. A partial list of Schenley whiskeys that were available in the post–World War II period included:

- Ancient Age Straight Bourbon Whiskey, 90-proof, five years old
- Ancient Age Blended Straight Whiskey, 86-proof, eight years old

- Belmont Kentucky Straight Bourbon Whiskey, 86-proof, seven years old
- Cream of Kentucky Straight Bourbon Whiskey, 86-proof, four years old
- Gibson's Straight Bourbon Whiskey, 86-proof, four years old
- Golden Wedding Blended Straight Whiskey, 90-proof, five years old
- Green River Kentucky Straight Bourbon Whiskey, Bottled in Bond, 100-proof, five years old
- Green River Kentucky Straight Bourbon Whiskey, 86-proof, four years old
- I. W. Harper Kentucky Straight Bourbon Whiskey, Bottled in Bond, 100-proof, four years old
- I. W. Harper Kentucky Straight Bourbon Whiskey, 91.4-proof, four years old
- James E. Pepper Kentucky Straight Bourbon Whiskey, 90-proof, four years old
- James E. Pepper Kentucky Straight Bourbon Whiskey, Bottled in Bond, 100-proof, four years old
- Old Stagg Kentucky Straight Bourbon Whiskey, 86-proof, eight years old[2]

At the top of this list in Albert Blanton's opinion stood his pride and joy, the classic Old Stagg Kentucky Straight Bourbon Whiskey. By 1964, American consumers had purchased over 200 million 750-milliliter bottles, making Old Stagg the cornerstone brand to the Schenley whiskey empire.[3] In addition to Schenley's burgeoning portfolio of American whiskeys, the company also offered a wide array of rums, brandies, and gins to fit snugly into every household budget and liquor cabinet.

The domestic economic horizon seemed limitless as North America's four largest whiskey distillers, Schenley, Joseph E. Seagram, Hiram Walker, and National Distillers, all operated at peak capacity at distilleries on both sides of the Canada–United States border. Whiskeys that were not made by Schenley distilleries but sold well in this North

Thanks to you, we celebrate our 2,000,000ᵗʰ barrel of Top Kentucky Bourbon.

OLD STAGG

Never before has one Kentucky distillery produced the incredible total of 2,000,000 barrels of fine bourbon. That's over 13 *billion* drinks in 20 years

—thanks to you! Your appreciation of Old Stagg's consistent quality has made it America's largest-selling straight Kentucky bourbon.

Placed in America's first and only one-barrel bonded warehouse—this historic barrel of Old Stagg will patiently age and mellow for six long years.

Next time you're near Frankfort, Ky., home of Old Stagg, come and see this unique exhibit of the distiller's art. Old Stagg will welcome you!

OLD STAGG

EVERY MELLOW DROP

NOW **6** YEARS OLD

NO INCREASE IN PRICE! / STILL ONLY $0⁰⁰ PINT $0⁰⁰ 4/5 QT.

America's Largest-Selling Kentucky Bourbon

KENTUCKY STRAIGHT BOURBON WHISKEY • EVERY DROP 6 YEARS OLD 86 PROOF • ©1953, THE STAGG DISTILLING CO., FRANKFORT, KENTUCKY

Old Stagg print advertisement from 1953

American whiskey heyday included Old Crow, Ten High, Four Roses, Early Times, Jim Beam, and Old Hickory. In 1953, with Kentucky whiskey sales brisk throughout the United States, the George T. Stagg Distillery celebrated the production of its two millionth barrel of Old Stagg following the repeal of Prohibition. To celebrate the occasion, Rosenstiel ordered the building of a new warehouse at Leestown, Warehouse V. The Stagg compound continued to grow as plant manager Orville Schupp and his chief assistant Elmer T. Lee kept the whiskeys flowing and the workers busy.

But all was not a bed of roses in the hopeful 1950s. In a rare instance of Rosenstiel stumbling and making a blunder, he erroneously predicted that the length of the Korean War would exceed that of World War II. Clinging to this hunch, he had ramped up production at his distilleries to be prepared for the possibility of another post-war boom. That never occurred, however, since the Korean War lasted just a shade over three years from June of 1950 to July of 1953. Throughout the early to mid-1950s with Schenley's whiskey stocks running high at startling levels of overcapacity in all its plants and warehouses, Rosenstiel spent significant amounts of time and effort in Washington, D.C., buttonholing members of the federal government to restructure the nation's bonding period retroactively for whiskey matured from 8 to 20 years. Rosenstiel did this in order to release older whiskeys within the bounds of the law for the express purpose of relieving the tax burden to Schenley.[4] In other words, he needed to unload hundreds of thousands of gallons of whiskey to avoid paying the taxes on them as they sat in the Schenley aging warehouses. Rosenstiel's lobbying efforts did in time come to fruition in July 1959 when the laws were bent to his desire.[5]

As a result of this legal turnaround, Schenley's wordy advertisements for their older American whiskeys were plastered across the nation's newspapers, roadside billboards, and in popular magazines, like *Look*, *Life*, and *The Saturday Evening Post*. One print advertisement released from Schenley read, "Proudly presented for the first time since Repeal: Bottled in Bond Old Schenley Kentucky Bourbon Whiskey – Full Eight 8 Years Old – It took eight long years to bring it back . . . and each year it got better and better and better!"[6] Eventually, Schenley's whiskey stocks depleted as America and the world welcomed a new American president in 1960, the former U.S. Senator from Massachusetts John Fitzgerald Kennedy.

Lewis S. Rosenstiel: The Supreme Commander

In today's verbiage, spiked with political correctness, when one describes another person of difficult, even malicious personality, one can with some latitude characterize him or her as being "complicated." That is our contemporary manner of conveying with a spoonful of politeness and a dollop of irony that the individual in question is either woefully misunderstood or spiteful or, worst of all, downright nasty. "Ben is, well, how can I best say it? Complicated. Yeah, Ben is complicated." This sort of feeble, flaccid word play has become our modern way of saying, "Everyone, beware of Ben." That being one of the linguistic styles of our day, it is acceptable then to state without hesitation that Lewis S. Rosenstiel, the sometimes fierce and other times benevolent alpha-lion of Schenley Distilling Corporation, was *deeply complicated*.

Upon learning more about Rosenstiel's life story, cynics might claim that measuring him up against, say, his most revered employee Albert Bacon Blanton might be akin to comparing Darth Vader to Obi-Wan Kenobi. And, in fact, to some degree that flight of fancy would be unfair since Blanton and Rosenstiel lived their lives in vastly different worlds, one the modest, creative local hero who with quiet diligence fought local battles for his distillery and community, the other the swashbuckling, sometimes terrifying captain of industry who brawled in bare-knuckle fashion in the international corporate alleyways.

But before we delve into the bottomless black hole of his complex personality that led Schenley and the distilleries at the old Leestown site to majestic triumphs, we should initially give Lewis Solon Rosenstiel, born in Cincinnati, Ohio, on July 21, 1891, his due. Rosenstiel was a businessman of legendary adeptness, a peerless company leader, and as genuine and acute a beverage industry visionary as Joseph E. Seagram's Samuel

Bronfman. As the commanding and demanding chairman of the board of Schenley Distillers Corporation of 350 Fifth Avenue, New York City, he was admired for his apparent belief that each Schenley employee was a vital and respected part of the team, irrespective of their title. Whether this public posture was a charade or not, one could never really ascertain since Rosenstiel gave little away in terms of confidences, save to a chosen few, some of whom would never be hailed as model citizens.

But, with the clarity of retrospection, what is evident after over 70 years is that his internal company programs of outreach to Schenley employees were superbly crafted and effective in rousing company pride. Rosenstiel convincingly talked at length in letters, speeches, interviews, and conversations about the "Schenley Family." In no sphere was this more evident than in the slick intercompany publication, the *Schenley News*. The statement declaring, "Published monthly at Cincinnati, Ohio for all the employees of Schenley Industries, Inc. and its subsidiaries" was prominently positioned in the masthead located in the first pages of every edition.

When one thumbs through several issues of the *Schenley News* published between the period of 1950 to 1960 as I did, one can't help but be struck by all the positive, upbeat articles featuring smiling employees at all levels of the company, from maintenance workers at the George T. Stagg and James E. Pepper distilleries to key executives meeting in the Empire State Building in New York. The stories unfolded, one after another, about the personal accomplishments, job changes and promotions, fund-raising events, and "homey" features that with remarkable frequency focused on recent births, company softball games, retirement parties, and pictures from family vacations. Reports that touted company acquisitions, new brand releases, and even financial data ("Grain purchased 1933–1963, 270 million dollars!") filled each issue's pages. The print and billboard advertisements for the numerous whiskey brands of that era were also printed, such as the clever one for whiskey brands Old Charter and Ancient Age bourbons that read, "Some day they'll be back . . . These fine Kentucky straight whiskies are now aging for your future enjoyment . . . aging so that you can be assured of the continuous superb quality—each with its own distinctive character unchanged." Or, the ad with the clear directive that ran up the side, "The Height of Quality – I.W. HARPER The Gold Medal Whiskey, REMEMBER . . . More Sales, More Production, More Work."[7] Rosenstiel was a master of subliminal messaging.

Acknowledging how mechanical and frosty much of the corporate environment has become around the globe since the 1950s, it is simple to perceive that the *Schenley News* was a stroke of Rosenstiel's directional genius. It effectively promoted his concept of the "team," the Schenley Family, which, it deserves to be pointed out, was made up of women and men of all races and age groups. Through the glossy vehicle of the *Schenley News*, everyone at Schenley was involved in company business. Every employee was invested with a tangible stake in the direction of the company and its welfare. Most everything, by all appearances, was out on the table. How was that so? Easy; because it said so in the *Schenley News*. In the final analysis, Rosenstiel's *Schenley News* turned out to be a brilliant tactical move, the glue that instilled company-wide loyalty and pride.

Yet, for all of this organizational ebullience, how many Schenley insiders were privy to Lewis Rosenstiel's elusive and, by many accounts, disturbing dark side? Except for a few close associates, virtually no one. Rosenstiel's life has been described as "colorful," but that glosses over much of the stark reality. Yes, his drive, work ethic, and vision made Schenley a major player of beverage alcohol in the post-Prohibition and post–World War II decades. At one point in the late 1950s and early 1960s, Schenley Industries accounted for almost one quarter of all the spirits, beers, and wines sold in the United States. That success made Rosenstiel a multimillionaire. Married five times, Rosenstiel resided on an enormous 1,500-acre estate in tony Greenwich, Connecticut.

But Rosenstiel, notorious for having a ferocious and lightning-quick temper, was someone you did not mess with. A little known fact as time has marched on was that he was indicted in 1929 during Prohibition for bootlegging, but was never convicted.[8] Like Seagram CEO Samuel Bronfman, Rosenstiel was long suspected of dealing with organized crime figures during the dry years of 1920–1933, in particular, with the Italian-American and Jewish-American gangs that together formed the so-called "National Crime Syndicate."[9] The U.S. Senate Special Committee to

Investigate Crime in Interstate Commerce, also known as the Kefauver Committee, convened in 1950 and 1951 to scrutinize not just the organized crime gangs, but also the suspected business people who may have aided and abetted the Crime Syndicate, beginning in the early years of Prohibition. Among the foremost businessmen implicated through the testimony of several syndicate mobsters were Samuel Bronfman and Lewis Rosenstiel.

While Senator Estes Kefauver and his committee failed to conclusively prove their allegations after conducting hearings in 14 cities and calling scores of witnesses, most with conveniently timed memory lapses, the information that did emerge was not flattering for anyone, including Rosenstiel and his friend, FBI Director J. Edgar Hoover.[10] As the nation's top policeman, Hoover had suspiciously rejected the idea of a crime syndicate for decades. Then under oath facing the Special Committee, Hoover retracted his numerous earlier claims, admitting publicly that such an organization had and still did exist.

Years later, through testimony from Rosenstiel's fourth wife Susan Kaufman, it was learned that Hoover may have been quiet about organized crime due to being blackmailed, possibly by Rosenstiel, who according to Kaufman hosted wild parties held at New York's Plaza Hotel in Suite 233 featuring male (read: underage boy) prostitutes.[11] The parties, which occurred often in order to blackmail people in positions of power and influence, were audio recorded by Rosenstiel, according to Kaufman. The tapes' release would have destroyed careers, including that of the FBI director. J. Edgar Hoover, who was widely acknowledged by the 1950s to be a closeted cross-dresser who preferred to be called "Mary," was a man of unusual carnal appetites. Ironically, Hoover himself was a notorious blackmailer who possessed files with unsavory data that he held over the heads of many politicians, entertainers, and public figures, including reportedly Richard Nixon and Francis Cardinal Spellman, the archbishop of New York.[12] Whether or not Rosenstiel "had the goods" on Hoover is debatable since their relationship, at least in public, lasted until Hoover's death in 1972.

In February of 1971, the *New York Times* ran a story titled, "Ex-Head of Schenley Industries Is Linked to 'Crime Consortium.'" Reported the article, "A Congressional investigator testified yesterday that Lewis

Rosenstiel . . . was part of a 'consortium' with underworld figures that bought liquor in Canada during Prohibition and sold it illegally in the United States . . . the consortium bought the liquor from Samuel Bronfman, the founder of Seagram Distillers."[13]

Further testimony by Susan Kaufman claimed that she possessed photographs of Rosenstiel and famed mobster Meyer Lansky taken at parties hosted by Rosenstiel. A reporter for the *Philadelphia Inquirer* confirmed the existence of the pictures. Another of Rosenstiel's nefarious chums was attorney Roy M. Cohn, who reportedly viewed Rosenstiel as a father figure. Cohn, widely suspected of being a pedophile, made headlines in the early 1950s for being a key member of Senator Joseph McCarthy's team during the ill-fated hearings on communist activity in the entertainment business. The triangular kinship between Rosenstiel, Hoover, and Cohn frequently set tongues wagging both in New York City and Washington, D.C., as to their intentions. *Life* Magazine reported once that Cohn, like Meyer Lansky, addressed Rosenstiel as "Supreme Commander" and Rosenstiel dubbed Cohn "Field Commander."[14] If this was true, the question could fairly be asked, *Supreme Commander of what?*

The last chapter of the Rosenstiel-Cohn saga came full circle when Cohn was disbarred by the state of New York, in part, because of his illegal attempt to include his name as co-executor in the will of Lewis Rosenstiel. Reported the *New York Times* on June 25, 1976, "A Dade County [Florida] probate judge declared here today that Roy M. Cohn had tricked the late Lewis S. Rosenstiel into signing a disputed codicil naming Mr. Cohn a trustee of the liquor magnate's $75 million estate."[15] Cohn's law career never recovered. Nevertheless, that career setback did not render Cohn toothless. He continued to influence and carouse with the rich, unsavory, and infamous until his death from AIDS in 1986, including the brash real estate mogul who would later become the divisive 45th president of the United States, Donald J. Trump.[16]

Noted whiskey blogger Chuck Cowdery in 2019, "Cohn's gambit failed. Rosenstiel was luckier. Despite many salacious rumors, he is mostly remembered as a successful business leader and generous philanthropist."[17] Cowdery's crisp viewpoint is true. The claim could also be made that Rosenstiel's legacy, once in jeopardy, had been tidied up over the ensuing decades by an industry anxious, once and for all, to close the books on its dubious past, a past rife with suspicious yet acknowledged associations between the captains of beverage alcohol and the warlords of organized crime. Lewis Rosenstiel died at the age of 84 in Miami Beach, Florida in January of 1976.[18]

How does one assess in the temporal balance someone else's life, in this case Lewis Rosenstiel's? A life that included, on the positive side, the creation of a hugely successful national beverage alcohol conglomerate that employed thousands of people and his generous philanthropy that approached $100 million directed to the betterment of hospitals and universities and then, on the negative side, the hosting of bawdy gatherings at which he is alleged to have recorded the intimate interactions of high-profile people frolicking with under-age children to gain their allegiance, the alleged relations involving bootlegging with vicious underworld criminals, and the clandestine activities and warped relationships that were at their best wicked and amoral and at their worst criminal? One cannot and should not judge Rosenstiel with absolute certainty because as the record depicts never was he convicted of any crime. Yet, the emphatic cacophony of sordid rumors, official investigations, and credible accusations from multitudinous sources does make one pause. What *can* be determined about the man who led Schenley Industries and the George T. Stagg Distillery from Prohibition until December of 1982 when the distillery was sold was that Lewis Rosenstiel led far more than just an interesting existence. He led a complicated life.

13

"Show Up Next Monday Morning . . ."

RESPECTED AS THE consummate whiskey professional by his peers throughout Kentucky, Orville Schupp departed the George T. Stagg Distillery in 1957. At the request of the parent company Schenley Distillers, Incorporated, Schupp accepted the lead position as plant manager of Schenley's large industrial distillery complex in Lawrenceburg, Indiana, which today is known as MGPI of Indiana, LLC. There, he worked on whiskey brands such as I.W. Harper, J.W. Dant, Old Stagg, and Ancient Age for a decade before advancing to being president of Schenley Distillers, starting in 1967. Over his tenure at the Frankfort distilleries, Schupp had developed a close working relationship with Albert Blanton, who from their earliest years together viewed Schupp as the most likely candidate to replace him. Upon Blanton's departure from the George T. Stagg Distillery following 14 successful years of plant and brand management, Schupp recommended that Elmer T. Lee become his successor as plant manager. In 1969, Lee was handed that responsibility. No one knew at the time nor could they have guessed how critically important promoting Lee would be to the history of domestic whiskey-making in the second half of the twentieth century and beyond.

Elmer Tandy Lee, born in 1919 near Frankfort, was a soft-spoken, memorably modest World War II veteran. He served as a crewmember flying B-29 aircraft, the massive, four-propeller heavy bombers nicknamed "Superfortresses." In the late stages of the war he participated in bombing raids, flying from Guam to Japan. Returning to Kentucky from action in the Pacific theatre in 1946, Lee took advantage of the G.I. Bill, which assisted in paying for the college education of war veterans. Attending the University of Kentucky, Lee graduated in 1949 at the age of 30 with a degree in chemical engineering.[1]

As pivotal as his promotion to plant manager would become, Lee's beginning at the George T. Stagg Distillery was of itself worthy of a minor tale to be told over dessert with a shot of bourbon. Orville Schupp was remembered in whiskey circles for taking particular delight in retelling the story of how the unassuming, quiet young man, named Elmer T. Lee, was first rejected in 1949 by Albert Blanton following a brief initial interview with Schupp. Blanton, after a short discussion with Schupp concerning the young chemical engineer's prospects, politely informed Lee, "Son, we're not hiring any hands today." As Lee walked from the plant office, Schupp would recall, he called after him and said, "Show up next Monday morning and we'll find something for you."

Since the distillery was located near his house, Lee complied the following Monday. Clearly, Schupp, to his credit, recognized something notable in Lee that triggered a positive response that would overrule Blanton's decision. As it happened, Lee worked at the distillery until 1985 when he retired with the title of Master Distiller Emeritus. But even after he retired, Lee habitually showed up at the plant, actually most Tuesdays, to continue his personal hunt for the perfect bourbon as well as to greet visitors and well-wishers. As Lee himself commented on his hiring to me in Frankfort when I interviewed him in the winter of 1994 nine years after his retirement, "Orville [Schupp] saw, I think, immediately how badly I wanted to work . . . eager just to work, fresh out of university, I needed a job. I knew next to nothing about distilling, except that I liked bourbon."

Throughout the 1950s and 1960s, Lee earned the status of becoming an irreplaceable member of the distillery operation at the old Leestown crossing spot. Life at the George T. Stagg Distillery throughout the 1960s was made hectic with whiskey production as American consumers continued their unbridled love affair with bourbons and blended whiskeys of the inexpensive variety. In 1964, the American whiskey industry received a nominal boost from the U.S. Congress when it in somewhat opaque language declared, "Bourbon whiskey is a distinctive product of the United States . . . it is the sense of Congress that the recognition of Bourbon whiskey . . . be brought to the attention of the appropriate agencies." Okay. Yet, when you carefully read the wording of the Congressional resolution the language is indefinite and vague. Soon after the public release of the resolution, that nebulous wording somehow morphed into the more wishful interpretation, "Congress declares Bourbon as America's native spirit," which in fact the 1964 Congressional resolution never stipulated.[2] Decades on, one still hears the ritualized verbal drumbeat that Congress made "Bourbon America's native spirit" from writers, bloggers, and other self-professed experts with Twitter accounts who have not taken the time to ingest the fine print from 1964. There is also a camp of theorists that believes that no less a shadowy puppet-master than Lewis Rosenstiel was behind the lobbying pressure applied to Congress to make some sort of upbeat gesture that would propel whiskey sales forward. Whatever the semantics, whatever the cause, whiskey production was throttled up to passing gear levels as stocks grew by the thousands of barrels each month throughout the middle tier states.

By the middle of the 1970s, whiskey inventories were burgeoning in warehouse after warehouse all across the lower Ohio River Valley. In Kentucky alone a reported 8.5 million barrels were shoehorned into warehouses.[3] Then the unthinkable happened when the case sales of clear-as-rainwater vodka cruised past those figures of domestic whiskey in the statistical fast lane. Headlines in 1976 business sections of small and big market newspapers screamed things like: "The Best Selling Spirits Now? VODKA!" and "Bourbon No Longer No. 1 Liquor in USA!"

In the unsettling effect of a major generational shift in consumer taste preferences, the restive crowd born in the post-war Baby Boom era of

1945–1964 became enamored with the transparent spirit that "Leaves You Breathless," as Smiroff Vodka advertisements claimed in magazine after magazine advertisement. The rebellious young adults of the late 1960s and early 1970s also fancied beer, marijuana, hashish, and Gallo Hearty Burgundy more than American whiskeys as whiskeys in general came to reflect images, in their view, of the World War II generation – in other words, their pitifully "square" parents and grandparents. The James B. Beam Company, makers of the number-one bourbon at the time, Jim Beam, made an awkward attempt at confronting the generational divide head-on with a see-through advertising campaign that was tellingly titled, "Generation gap? Jim Beam never heard of it."[4] Demonstrating the marketing department textbook example of exquisite tone deafness, the series of Jim Beam bourbon ads featuring past-their-sell-by-date celebrities, such as actor Bette Davis, actor-director Orson Welles, and movie director John Huston, only illustrated how little Beam was paying attention to the evolving marketplace atmosphere.

Just as embarrassing was Brown-Forman's feeble attempt, the curiously named Frost 8-80, to curry favor with 20-something vodka drinkers by spending untold amounts of R&D money and resources on creating a colorless eight-year-old Pennsylvania rye that tasted just as its appearance promised it would: totally void of character. That knucklehead concept, after which marketing heads must have rolled like bowling balls looking for a strike at Lebowski's Alleys, was dead on arrival as bottles blanketed with dust were yanked from retail shelves a mere 12 months after its release.[5]

The trend in consumer preference by the late 1970s was painfully clear. The "Old" American whiskey guard of Old Crow, Old Taylor, Old Forester, Old Grand Dad, Old Stagg, Old Hickory, and Old Fitzgerald was being replaced by vodkas with snappy Russian- or Swedish-sounding names, like Smirnoff, Popov, Stolichnaya, Absolut, and Georgi, which were fueled by ad campaigns that featured the era's hippest people, like singer Eartha Kitt, actor Julie Newmar, late-night television host Steve Allen, comedian Woody Allen, and *Tonight Show* host Johnny Carson. Through their enormous success in the 1950s and 1960s, the American whiskey industry by the mid-1970s had become calcified, too self-satisfied in maintaining the status quo to innovate, and too preoccupied with counting net profits to entertain progressive new ideas to keep up with the times. In the seeming blink of a cat's eye, three factors upended the domestic whiskey industry in the 1970s: the industry's self-inflicted, top-heavy inventory position, based on the belief that their whiskeys would always be favored; the whiskey producers' inability to progress with the times and advance from the 1950s business models; and maybe the most dangerous, its hubris.

In 1977 and 1978, questions were flying like bats from a cave in the carpeted boardrooms and hushed hallways of America's whiskey empires, most prominently, those of whiskey-heavy Schenley Industries, Brown-Forman, Jim Beam, and National Distillers. How could vodka, that insipid unaged spirit that only in 1950 accounted for a measly 40,000 case sales total, surpass domestic whiskey sales a quarter-century later? How could this colorless, odorless (at least according to the U.S. government) spirit with subversive sounding names triumph over our aromatic and lovingly matured-in-barrels native spirit? Hey, didn't Congress pass that resolution? And, maybe most perversely, how could the vodka martini catapult in popularity when the old-fashioned and the whiskey sour cocktails could still be made with good old rye or smooth-tasting bourbon?

But, on American whiskey's bleak horizon came free-falling sales results in the 1980s. In addition to vodka's ascending popularity, the gradual rise of Scotland's idiosyncratic whiskies, known collectively as single malts, emerged in the marketplace. Blended Scotch whiskies had since the 1930s been part of the distilled spirits mural that painted the continental wall of North America. Members of the American military stationed in Scotland and England during World War II had taken a liking to Scotch whisky blends, those easy drinking whiskies comprised of soft grain and distinctive single malt whiskies. From San Francisco to Boston, brands like Dewar's White Label, J&B Rare, Cutty Sark, Vat 69, and Black & White blended Scotches had by 1950 become commonplace throughout the nation's bars, taverns, restaurants, and clubs.

But Scotland's rarer single malt whiskies, the weird-sounding, intense tasting libations made only from 100 percent malted barley in onion-shaped copper pot stills at a single distillery, were about to breach the commercial shoreline of the land of the free. Though only 27 single malt whiskies were available globally in 1980, most sold in Great Britain, the following year 49 were sent to market. By the time that *Auld Lang Syne* was being sung through the haze of champagne on December 31, 1989, 104 single malts could be purchased in the British Isles.[6]

To loosen the first pebbles of the Scotch single malt landslide in America, just four weeks earlier on Sunday, December 3, 1989, the Sunday magazine of the *New York Times* ran a full-color, 28-page special section devoted solely to Scotch whisky, called *Scotch Whisky – A Consumer Guide.*[7] Coverage of Scotch whisky in American magazines and newspapers steadily blossomed in the wake of the *Times* magazine coverage, stoking public and liquor trade interest. Due to their patrons' requests, retail liquor stores and finer restaurants and bars across America began stocking single malt whiskies from the Glenfiddich (*glen-fi-dick*), the Glenlivet (*glen-liv-it*), and Glenmorangie (*glen-MORE-ran-gee*) distilleries. The single malts from the Macallan distillery would soon join them. In the international whiskey sweepstakes, the trumpet had sounded to start the race that continues today.

The market dominance of vodka and the sudden emergence of Scotland's most elegant and mythical whiskies, coupled with the American whiskey surfeit, gave birth to grave and justifiable concern in America's distilleries. Yet, as members of the American whiskey complex woke up on January 1, 1990, there was after two decades of despair, a pinpoint beacon of light, a flashing spark that had been ignited six years prior in a humid warehouse located near where centuries before herds of buffalo had trampled the Kentucky River shallows.

The Shot of Bourbon Heard 'Round the World

With the retirement of Lewis Rosenstiel in 1968,[8] who divested himself of all his Schenley shares, Schenley Industries started to drift off course in the absence of his iron will and stalwart leadership. The introduction of a new line-up of so-called "light" whiskeys in 1972[9] was met with the sound of one hand clapping. By confusing the drinking public and their own consumer base with the descriptor "light," the company ended up sitting on stocks of Schenley American Blend, Melrose Rare Blended Light Whiskey, Red Satin by Schenley American Blended Light Whiskey, and Three Feathers Superior American Light Whiskey as they piled up, pallet-by-pallet, in Schenley warehouses. By the time eight years later that Rosenstiel died, Schenley Industries was a muddled behemoth with stagnant sales and obsolete marketing concepts. To counter some of the imbalance of their top-heavy whiskey portfolio, the decision came down from the Empire State Building to sell off some of their properties, including their crown jewel, the George T. Stagg Distillery in Frankfort and its primary prestige brand, Ancient Age Straight Bourbon.

In late 1982, two New York businessmen, Ferdie Falk and Robert Baranaskas, former executives at Fleischmann's Distilling Company, made a pitch to buy Schenley's Old Charter brand. Schenley refused to sell off Old Charter, but instead offered Falk and Baranaskas the George T. Stagg Distillery along with the rights to sell its flagship brand Ancient Age.[10] In early 1983, they took ownership of the fabled George T. Stagg Distillery. Falk and Baranaskas then renamed the company Age International.[11] A major asset of the George T. Stagg Distillery was Elmer T. Lee, the experienced plant manager. While Lee's disarming demeanor most likely charmed them from their first meeting, his encyclopedic knowledge of distilling and barrel maturation may have given the impression that he knew the worth of every barrel in every warehouse. In addition, Lee was the picture of what a Kentucky distiller should be, from his ever-present Scottish flat cap to his easy, casual, gentlemanly manner. The fact that Lee, like the distillery's namesake, was keenly aware of the location of the plant's foremost bourbon barrels had to deeply impress the new owners, who were anxious to look beyond domestic sales for top-tier bourbon whiskeys.

Aware of the growing mystique associated with Scotland's single malts, the decline of American whiskey at home, and of Japan's expanding economy, Falk and Baranaskas asked Lee to gather the best barrels of mature bourbon from the Age International warehouses for a possible new brand that would sell at a premium price. Hearing the new directive, Lee related to Falk and Baranaskas the story of how Albert Blanton would task trusted employees with finding the best barrels of older bourbons with a minimum age of eight years from the top two floors of his favorite warehouse, the metal-sided Warehouse H, and then bring samples to him to taste. After choosing the finest old barrels of bourbon from the fifth and sixth floors, he had the team bottle them for his own pleasure as well as his closest friends. Blanton had always favored the undiluted, full-strength whiskeys from those floors. And, who would know better?

Baranaskas, in particular, liked the story and thereby instructed Lee, "We're going to go with that and we want you to select the bourbons that go into this brand. We're going to name it Blanton." In Elmer T. Lee's own words from his personal journal written in 1990, "Blanton Bourbon was born in 1983 in the minds of Mr. Bob Baranaskas, Mr. Ferdie Falk, & Elmer T. Lee. As a culmination of a legend & several facts as related to Mr. Baranaskas & Mr. Falk by Elmer T. Lee in 1983 . . ."[12] In the autumn of 1984, the inaugural shipment of Blanton's Single Barrel Kentucky Straight Bourbon Whiskey arrived in Japan. The package was unlike anything seen before in American whiskey, with each short, round bottle carrying a card saying, "The finest bourbon in the world comes from a single barrel." Every bottle also sported details identifying the barrel number and the originating warehouse, lending an air of authenticity. Young Japanese whiskey drinkers responded by purchasing whatever Blanton's they could find, similar to their reaction years earlier to I.W. Harper Kentucky Straight Bourbon.

Blanton's would in time go on to become a breakthrough in the history, not just of American whiskey but in the annals of American spirits, since never before had a full strength, super-premium whiskey from a single cask been offered by any Kentucky distiller. With Elmer T. Lee's inspired epiphany to create Blanton's Single Barrel Kentucky Straight Bourbon Whiskey, the international whiskey landscape would eventually be forever altered. For the first time, the crème de la crème of American whiskey could be discussed in the same conversation with the best of Scotland's fabled single malt whiskies. After 1984, it was game on . . . well, almost.

"Glad to see Libby & be home . . ."

The reception that Blanton's Single Barrel received was initially more favorable in faraway Japan, which was undergoing a social revolution among young adults, than it was at home. Bottles of Blanton's in Japan were found selling in Tokyo and Osaka for the Japanese yen equivalent of $100. In the United States, it sold for $35 for the 750-milliliter bottle that was capped with horse-and-jockey stoppers. Thirty-five dollars in the mid-1980s was an astronomical amount for consumers to plunk down on a retail counter top when standard brands of bourbon were purchased nationwide from $7 to $10 per bottle. Lee himself admitted in his journal of Blanton's early sales numbers in the United States, "It didn't do much the first year."

With sales in the United States sluggish, Baranaskas and Falk arranged for taste tests to be conducted "blind" between Blanton's Single Barrel and the other new up-and-comer, Maker's Mark Bourbon, created by Bill Samuels. Blanton's won against Maker's Mark in several annual blind tastings, though Samuels cried "foul" because the Maker's bottles were bought at random liquor stores while the Blanton's Single Barrel was bottled especially for that event. That said, Baranaskas and Falk did achieve at least one goal: people in the media were suddenly talking about Blanton's Single Barrel as more stories about premium American whiskeys and their potential started making the rounds by the mid-1990s.

Elmer T. Lee retired from Age International in 1985 to spend more time with Libby, his wife. He remained on the payroll, however, in an advisory role. Sales remained slow not just for Blanton's Single Barrel but for all American whiskeys into the early 1990s. To illustrate domestic whiskey's malaise, in 1991 whiskeys with an American origination point belly-flopped to a dismal 15.6 million cases, the lowest categorical total since Prohibition.[13]

In the meantime, the majority of the Kentucky whiskey producers stayed aloof to the idea of high-priced whiskeys while in the midst of a cyclical slump. One exception was the lovably irascible and blunt master distiller at Jim Beam, Booker Noe, who introduced barrel strength, blow-the-toupee-off-your-pate Booker's Bourbon and the Beam Small Batch

Collection at the tail end of the 1980s. Another exception was master distiller Jimmy Russell at Wild Turkey, who followed suit with the release of super-premium, cask-strength Rare Breed Kentucky Straight Bourbon in 1991. To help tweak the public discussion of single barrel bourbon, Age International itself with Elmer T. Lee's guidance introduced three more single barrel bourbons, namely Rock Hill Farms (named after a home owned by Albert Blanton), Hancock's Reserve, and Elmer T. Lee, to honor the former plant manager's long career. Sales nonetheless remained listless.

Then in the summer of 1990, Baranaskas had a brainstorm. He approached Age International's retired/consulting distiller with a proposition. Wrote Lee in his journal, dated July 1990, "Bob Baranaskas & Joe Darmand talked to me about doing promotional work for the Blanton Bourbon Brand, after discussion with Libby I agreed. Bob agreed verbally to increase my consultant's fee from $600/mo. To $1,000 per month starting with July, 1990 . . . An agreement was executed (Joe Darmand signing for Age International) in Dec. 1990. Original of agreement in State National Bank, Fkt, KY. (East Branch) Lock-Box. Copy in my basement desk."[14]

This arrangement between Lee and Age International began a decade-long marathon of travel for the supposedly retired distiller that had him visiting markets across North America, Japan, and the British Isles, among other places. As evidenced by his meticulously kept journal, Lee stopped in at scores of prominent liquor stores (Sam's in Chicago, Morrell and Company and Sherry-Lehman in New York), bars (The Rainbow Room in New York), clubs, and restaurants to talk about single barrel bourbon; he hosted hundreds of tasting events and dinners for groups of writers, for gatherings of dentists (February 4, 2004), for wine aficionado groups, for university clubs, for liquor distributors, at the offices of magazines and newspapers. He signed bottles at trade fairs (Big Smoke, Whisky-Fest, Wine & Spirits Wholesalers of America conventions), the Bourbon Festival, at golf tournaments, at country music jamborees. Lee was interviewed on local radio programs more times than he could account for. He conducted master classes on bourbon and was a guest bartender in London, Las Vegas, Chicago, San Francisco, Boston, New York, and numerous other cities.

Master Distiller Emeritus Elmer T. Lee

At first, as Lee reported, the crowds were small, with "tonight with 12–14 nice people." As the years rolled by, Lee's detailed journal entries revealed a steady attendance increase with each passing year, as audiences swelled to 30, 50, 100, 125, even 200 people per event. He had the habit of describing dinners he attended and what specifically he ate and of his many flying adventures as he took pains in recounting the model of the jets he flew in, the flight delays and cancellations and the airports he roamed. He wrote with admirable kindness about the people who accompanied him and with whom he met for the first time, even when he had to be dog-weary, or as Lee himself would describe it, "very pooped in hotel room tonight."

When he was at home in Frankfort, with his celebrity rising, his schedule would frequently find him at the distillery, making the rounds and answering questions from journalists. One of my favorite entries in Lee's journal is from February 24, 1994. It reads, "Mr. Paul Pacult – writer with Spirits Magazine (Spirits Journal) from New York, N.Y. visited Ancient Age plant today . . . Is doing an article on Bourbon & it's history & lore in their magazine soon . . . he interviewed me at plant clubhouse. Toured him thru Whse H & Blanton Bottling. To plant lab for taste test . . . He left about 3:30PM to visit Jimmy Russell at Wild Turkey. He was at Beam's Booker Noe & Bill Samuel at Maker's Mark that morning. Nice person & no doubt will do a good bourbon article."[15]

Typical of Lee's journal were the closing remarks from a trip to Las Vegas, dated February 28, 1995, "Checked out of hotel at 11AM. Taxi to airport for a 1PM Delta non-stop airline trip to Cincinnati, Ohio Airport. Smooth flight. Arrived 8PM. Left parking lot about 9PM & drove home arriving 10:30PM tired & glad to see Libby & be home."[16]

Fighting declining sales in a difficult U.S. marketplace in the waning days of 1991, Falk and Baranaskas sold off 22.5 percent of Age International to Takara Shuzo Company, Ltd., the importer of Blanton's in Japan. Takara Shuzo also gained a 30-day right of refusal clause to acquire the remaining shares of Age International. Because Takara Shuzo at first showed zero interest in owning a Kentucky distillery, Falk and Baranaskas quietly approached Heublein, Inc., an American subsidiary of Great Britain's drinks giant Grand Metropolitan. Hours before a final deal was struck with Heublein, Takara Shuzo exercised its legal right of refusal and purchased for a sum of $20 million the remaining shares of Age International and then pivoted and sold them to Sazerac Company of New Orleans, who as stipulated in the agreement would continue to produce Blanton's at the George T. Stagg Distillery. Falk and Baranaskas retired from the business, having made millions from the sale.

The sale of Age International and the selling rights to Blanton's, Rock Hill Farms, Hancock's Reserve, and Elmer T. Lee to the Sazerac Company in 1992 from Takara Shuzo, which remains the owner of the four brands, did nothing to alter Lee's furious public appearance schedule. If anything, the itinerary became broader in scope for the 73-year-old supposedly retired master distiller emeritus following the takeover. The management at Sazerac, led by the dynamic young president Peter Bordeaux, understood the importance of having Lee continue to serve as the public spokesperson for the benefit of its whiskey brands. The long-game payoff of this genuine, engaging personality talking in person to groups of interested adults paid off, as sales and the recognition of Kentucky's premium whiskeys, in general, began to generate stronger sales by the mid-1990s.

To claim that Elmer T. Lee upheld with grace and dignity the Frankfort distillery whiskey man tradition established earlier by E.H. Taylor, Jr., George T. Stagg, Albert Blanton, and Orville Schupp is an exercise in gross understatement. Upon meeting him for the first time, Lee's amiable nature and easy smile put everyone at ease, but these homespun traits also concealed the razor-sharp intelligence and innate toughness of a former wartime bombardier. Commented the present public relations manager of Buffalo Trace Distillery, Amy Preske, who often traveled with Lee in his last years of promotional touring, "Elmer was tough. He mellowed in his later years. A couple of old-timers said that early on he could be a real S.O.B." Once he began addressing the complexities of the single barrel bourbons that he loved, the intricate barrel-aging methods he employed, and the warehouses that to him were cathedrals, the depth of Lee's genius was impossible to miss. Elmer T. Lee died in 2013 at the age of 93.

The Indelible Impact of American Whiskey's Greatest Generation

The reason why American whiskey – straight ryes, straight bourbons, American single malts, bottled-in-bond whiskeys, wheat whiskeys, and more – has reached its zenith in the first quarter of the twenty-first century is due in significant measure to a single generation of highly skilled twentieth-century distillers. These extraordinary maestros, 11 in number, answered the bell of change when it chimed during the period of the middle 1980s to just after the turn of the century. This proved to be an exceptional and unprecedented era of innovation and product quality realization in the annals of American whiskey production.

The following individuals are the legends of bourbon and American whiskey who ushered in the current boom years: Elmer T. Lee and Gary Gayheart of George T. Stagg (later Buffalo Trace Distillery); Booker Noe and Jerry Dalton of Jim Beam Brands (now Beam Suntory); Parker Beam of Heaven Hill Distilleries; Lincoln Henderson of Brown-Forman and later of Angel's Envy; Willie Pratt of Brown-Forman and later of Michter's; Jimmy Russell of Wild Turkey; Bill Samuels, Jr. of Maker's Mark; Jim Rutledge formerly of Four Roses; and Julian P. Van Winkle III of Pappy Van Winkle. Each participated in and contributed mightily to this astounding renaissance, the rebirth of an entire domestic industry that had been given up for dead in the 1970s, 1980s, and the first half of the 1990s. History shows with crystal clarity that through their whiskey output and successes, it was this group of down-home, easy-as-Sunday-morning visionaries that resurrected American whiskey during the fertile 20-year period spanning from 1985 to 2005.

A testament to their collective influence is experienced by whiskey lovers each day in 2021 as they swallow and savor top-drawer, world-class whiskeys like Woodford Reserve Double Oaked Bourbon, Four Roses Small Batch Bourbon, Pappy Van Winkle's Family Reserve 20-Year-Old Straight Bourbon, Blanton's Single Barrel Bourbon, Jim Beam Distillers Masterpiece Bourbon, Russell's Reserve Single Barrel Bourbon, Elijah Craig Barrel Proof Bourbon, Angel's Envy Cask Strength Bourbon, Parker's Heritage editions, the Buffalo Trace Antique Collection editions, Old Fitzgerald, the W.L. Weller portfolio, and Maker's Mark 46. These are just a few superb examples of the current American whiskey portfolio.

These remarkable distillers and their iconic whiskeys, in part, paved the way for skilled craft distillers and acclaimed mom-and-pop whiskey brands like FEW, Smooth Ambler, Low Gap, Dry Fly, Peerless, Westward, Breckenridge, High West, Treaty Oak, New Riff, Koval, Hillrock, Wyoming, Redemption, Union Horse, Clyde May's, Rogue, Copper Fox, Coppersea, Bardstown, Tuthilltown (also known as Hudson), Charbay, Leopold Bros, Stranahan's, Balcones, Journeyman, Corsair, Copperworks, Uncle Nearest, and many more to chart exciting new regions of sensory experience. If the first Golden Age of American whiskey happened in the late nineteenth century and the second Golden Age happened in the post–World War Two decades of the 1950s and 1960s, the post–World War II generation made all the right decisions in launching the present-day Golden Age of American whiskey.

Tonight, be certain to toast Elmer, Jimmy, Booker, Lincoln, Bill, Parker, Julian, Willie, Gary, Jerry, and Jim the next time you pour a glass of shimmering American whiskey. Wherever they are, they will appreciate and deserve the gesture.

14

Sazerac: The New Orleans Company and the Fabled Cocktail

ABOUT THE TIME in the late 1850s that Daniel Swigert was occupied building the first verifiable whiskey distillery at the Leestown site on the banks of the Kentucky River, a New Orleans bar, the Sazerac Coffee-House, was busy serving Crescent City residents and visitors distinctive coffees and alcoholic drinks that would make it famous, not just in the city but throughout the American South. During the nineteenth century, the concept of the New Orleans "coffee house" was the genteel equivalent of the rougher Chicago "tap room" or the raucous Boston "corner tavern" or the bawdy San Francisco "watering hole." In the 1850s, New Orleans coffee houses were crowded places of roaring community conviviality, where neighbors gathered to hear the latest news, to sip a coffee, to swap gossip, and perhaps to enjoy an elixir that was a tad stronger than a cup of java to kick off the day. How popular were the NOLA coffee houses in the nineteenth century? More than 200 of them were identified in the 1859 New Orleans city directory.[1]

In addition to the potent coffees made from deep brown beans sourced from Cuba and other Caribbean islands, coffee houses offered for sale as a matter of regional routine various types of distilled spirits, such as cognacs, rums, rye whiskeys, and gins. Then, there were the potion-like concoctions served up by the waxed mustachioed barkeeps, the cocktails that were comprised of calculated mixtures of spirits, bitters, juices, and tinctures. During the Civil War years, the coffees were often mixed with chicory root,[2] kind of like "stretching the soup," when shipping lanes from eastern cities to New Orleans were affected by the Union Army's blockade that ran from the Virginia coastline to the Mississippi Delta. If you know anything about the astringent taste of chicory root, it isn't a great leap then to project that establishments like the Sazerac Coffee-House were busy mixing cocktails, morning, noon, afternoon, and night.

The original name of the Sazerac Coffee-House was the Merchant's Exchange Coffee House. Sewell Taylor (no relation to E.H. Taylor, Jr.) first opened the business in 1840 at 13 Exchange Alley. It soon became the talk of New Orleans for its impressive 125-foot-long bar behind which worked up to a dozen bartenders.[3] The name was changed in 1852 to Sazerac Coffee-House when a gentleman named Aaron Bird bought it from Sewell Taylor. One of the most popular liquors that was available in the neighborhood coffee shops at that time was Sazerac de Forge et Fils Cognac. Established in 1782 in Limoges, France by Bernard Sazerac de Forge, the savory brandies of Sazerac de Forge were coveted throughout France, as well as in the eastern seaboard and southern tier states of the United States. Confirming Sazerac de Forge et Fils's presence in America is a notice that appeared in 1839 in the *Philadelphia National Gazette* newspaper that reads, "Brandy --- 40 half pipes 'Odard, Dupuy & Co.'s' brand—25 do dark colored, very old Sazerac brand---11 hhds, vintage of 1827, Sazerac. For sale by ROBERT ADAMS & Cp., 123 Walnut st."

Like so many instances involving beverage alcohol lore, theories abound about the renaming of the Sazerac Coffee-House and as to whether Aaron Bird's inspiration rose from his admiration of the French brandy or, as some people postulate, from the Sazerac cocktail that was said to be popular in the 1850s. This point has been up for debate for years among booze geeks, cocktail bloggers, and those 40-something men still living in their mother's basements. My own betting money lies with the line of thinking that Bird's inspiration was linked to Sazerac de Forge et Fils. My reasoning is born of the lack of documented evidence showing beyond any doubt that the Sazerac cocktail even existed prior to the last quarter of the 1800s. This viewpoint is bolstered by my colleagues, the noted cocktail historian and author David Wondrich and "King Cocktail" Dale DeGroff, who each believe that the Sazerac cocktail didn't, in fact, even make its first appearance until well after the 1850s, as it does not appear in any documentation until much later in 1899 as a mention in a fraternity journal. That being the most probable case, the timing then doesn't align cozily enough to affirm the cocktail theorists' beliefs.

Returning to what is germane, in 1860 Aaron Bird moved on from the coffee house business, selling the Sazerac Coffee-House to a John B. Schiller, the New Orleans agent for Sazerac de Forge et Fils. Nine years later, Schiller, who reportedly was in poor health, sold the establishment to one of the coffee house employees, his bookkeeper Thomas H. Handy, in 1870.[4] Wanting to place his own imprint on the property, Handy dropped the "coffee" from the name, calling it simply "Sazerac House."[5] Under Handy's nimble direction, the Sazerac House attracted the city's most prominent personalities and intriguing denizens. Described a reporter from the *New York Times* after one of the Houses' closings, ". . . one might see at any time a Judge, the Mayor of the City, perchance the Governor himself, and certainly a score of lesser dignitaries."[6]

One year after Handy's takeover, the famed bitters producer Antoine Peychaud joined Thomas H. Handy to form Thomas H. Handy & Company, which in 1873 became the exclusive importer of Sazerac de Forge et Fils. Handy also created Handy's Aromatic Cocktail Bitters. Some cocktail nerds theorize that Handy and Peychaud may have toyed with the first rudimentary incarnations of a Sazerac-like cocktail, but that is mere speculation. Made with a rye whiskey base and not cognac, the Sazerac cocktail had nothing to do with the famed coffee house located at 13 Exchange Alley. It likewise makes complete sense that the foundational spirit for the Sazerac cocktail was indeed rye whiskey rather than cognac since hardly any cognac was available in New Orleans or in the United States at all by the 1870s–1880s due to the French vineyards in the Charente *département* being decimated by the voracious *Phylloxera vastatrix* louse. So putting this superfluous matter to bed once and for all since there are more pertinent issues to discuss, the inspiration for the name of the Sazerac Coffee-House had to come courtesy of the French cognac producer Sazerac de Forge et Fils.

Meanwhile, the Thomas H. Handy & Company wobbled in 1878 under the weight of debt when Handy's personal assets suffered a major setback. Handy's net worth vanished when his investments in chancy railroad stocks skidded off the rails. As a result of his severe financial troubles, he was forced to dissolve Thomas H. Handy & Company and pass along the keys of the Sazerac House to a gentleman by the name of Vincent Micas, who for undisclosed reasons shut its doors in 1882. The building at 13 Exchange Alley was soon demolished. Even with that short-lived period of moderate success at Sazerac House though, Handy, who died in 1893, is remembered today by a highly visible straight rye whiskey that is part of Buffalo Trace Distillery's iconic Antique Collection of exclusive bourbons and ryes. We should all be so lucky.

After being rebuilt, the reopened Sazerac House was then operated by bartender and entrepreneur William "Billy" H. Wilkinson under the business name of Thomas H. Handy & Company. At the turn of the twentieth century, the company started peddling a new rye whiskey called Sazerac Rye. The company also had significant success selling a line of premixed and bottled cocktails, aptly named Sazerac Cocktails. A half dozen Sazerac Cocktail varieties – Holland Gin, Sherry, Vermouth, Martini, Tom Gin and Whiskey – were sold across the country.[7] Touted a print advertisement dated from 1901, "As Famous In New Orleans As The Mardi Gras. . .SAZERAC COCKTAILS – Nectar For The Gods. Pints. . .75¢ Quarts. . .1.50."[8] Sales of Nectar For The Gods were brisk until the start of Prohibition when, not surprisingly, the rye whiskey and the premixed cocktails were discontinued.

Hard times again rained down on Sazerac House as William H. Wilkinson died in 1904, a victim of tuberculosis. After Wilkinson's death, a former financial backer of Sazerac House William McQuoid and the company secretary Christopher O'Reilly resuscitated the business yet once more under the familiar title of the Thomas H. Handy & Company. In short order, the reorganized company operated the still-popular Sazerac House, slinging its cocktails and coffees. Soon thereafter, O'Reilly, as president, formally changed the name of the ownership entity to Sazerac Company.

Upon the repeal of Prohibition in 1933, the Sazerac Company began operating by importing and distributing spirits. The owners also opened a new bar and lunchroom at 300 Carondelet Street that served Sazerac cocktails for an agreeable price of 20 cents. The liquor side of Sazerac's business made money by offering private label bottlings to select customers throughout the state of Louisiana. Liquors with monikers such as Pride of Maryland Straight Rye Whiskey, Dog House Kentucky Straight Bourbon Whiskey, Pontchartrain Beach Whiskey, and Silver Lake Distilled Dry Gin kept Sazerac's ledgers well in the black ink. Pride of Maryland Straight Rye was the out-of-the-gate rye whiskey of choice for the Sazerac Cocktail.

Then in 1948, a competitor, the Magnolia Liquor Company owned by Stephen Goldring, purchased the Sazerac Company outright. In an article in the *New Orleans Times-Picayune* from 1948, Goldring asserted with conviction that, "The company [Sazerac] will be entirely concerned with bottling and wholesale distribution of alcoholic beverages, and tentatively plans to expand its facilities and sell its products nationwide within a year, he said."

Little did Stephen Goldring know three years after the end of World War II what fortunes were yet to come as his New Orleans-based company began a series of brand acquisitions that had the beverage industry talking. Four years after the purchase, the post-war decade when North American whiskey reigned as the undisputed category leader in the domestic marketplace, Sazerac and Goldring rolled the dice by introducing an inexpensive vodka brand, Taaka. Against the odds, Taaka went on to become successful in a whiskey era and remains a solid seller to this day, retailing in the $8–9 range.

Stephen Goldring, according to his son, William Goldring, the current CEO of Sazerac Company, was somewhat apprehensive about whiskey. Said William in an interview for a blog operated by Rouses Supermarkets, Louisiana's most prominent supermarket chain, "When I first got into this business, my father said, 'Bill, you never want to go into the bourbon business, because one day you're gonna wake up and you're going to own a lake full of bourbon, and you're not gonna know what to do with it, because people's tastes change.'" The irony now of course is that William Goldring's Sazerac Company owns Buffalo Trace Distillery, its crown jewel, along with several other whiskey distilleries, like A. Smith Bowman of Fredericksburg, Virginia, Glenmore in Owensboro, Kentucky, Barton 1792 in Bardstown, Kentucky, Popcorn Sutton in Newport, Tennessee, Boston Brands of Maine in Lewiston, Maine, and the Old Montreal Distillery in Montreal, Quebec, Canada, making it the most powerful and prolific source of bourbon and American whiskey in North America.

"Never thought of doing anything else"

William Goldring is a third-generation liquor business old hand who never considered entering any other industry. His grandfather Newman Goldring founded the family firm in 1898. Following three years at Tulane University, where he earned a Bachelor's Degree in Business, and then doing a worthwhile spell earning his spurs while working at Joseph E. Seagram & Sons in the northeast, Goldring returned home to New Orleans to pick up the mantel at Magnolia Company. In 1982, William succeeded his father Stephen as company president. By 1991 he had ascended to the post of chairman of the board at both Magnolia and Sazerac.

In the period before Sazerac purchased what is now the Buffalo Trace Distillery, Goldring had made a number of shrewd liquor brand acquisitions, including one from Seagram's that brought over brands such as Nikolai Vodka, Eagle Rare Kentucky Straight Bourbon, James Foxe Canadian Whisky, Carstairs Blended Whiskey, Dr. McGillicuddy's Liqueurs, Benchmark Bourbon, Fireball Whisky, and Crown Russe Vodka and Gin. Notable as pieces of whiskey trivia were Benchmark Bourbon and Eagle Rare Bourbon, as they were two of the last American whiskey brands to debut immediately prior to the cataclysmic bourbon collapse of the late 1960s.[9] Soon after, Goldring struck again, buying the spirits and wine company, Monsieur Henri.

Even in the wake of the visionary releases of Blanton's Single Barrel Bourbon, Booker's Bourbon, and Wild Turkey Rare Breed, the mid-1980s to mid-1990s continued to witness lackluster growth for American whiskeys. Even with its sterling history, the George T. Stagg Distillery in Frankfort was struggling to survive, producing a mere 12,000 barrels in 1995. By contrast, in 1973 the distillery produced a hefty 200,000 barrels. Its payroll in 1992 was down to 40 employees and much of the distillery machinery, warehouses, and buildings had seen better days. Yet, even in view of his father's earlier dire warning about treating bourbon as you would a nest of hornets in your birthday suit, William Goldring saw a glimmer of opportunity in the dilapidated distillery and its bourbon inventory at the old Leestown site. He would later explain, "We just figured bourbon was going to come back."

There was also the reality that this particular Kentucky distillery had an unmatched pedigree, touting a stellar roster of previous owners and legendary distillers that included industry icons like E.H. Taylor, Jr., George T. Stagg, Albert Blanton, Orville Schupp, and the recently retired, though still active, Elmer T. Lee. Lee's successor was Gary Gayheart, an able whiskey industry veteran who had gained previous experience at the Fleishmann Distilling Corporation in Owensboro and the Bernheim plant in Louisville. Though he was still able to produce small amounts of whiskey, primarily Ancient Age Bourbon, the lack of company resources prior to the purchase by Sazerac had tied Gayheart's hands.

And so armed solely with that seemingly meager aspiration that a bourbon comeback was imminent, the Sazerac Company of New Orleans, Louisiana, in 1992 bought the inventory of the George T. Stagg Distillery, a.k.a. Ancient Age Distillery. As a bonus the deal also included the distillery complex and its 113 acres in Frankfort, Kentucky. Said Goldring of his decision, "The distillery, after Prohibition, had a reputation for making the best whiskey in America." The whiskeys being produced with a recipe known as Mash Bill #1 were labeled as Benchmark Bourbon and Eagle Rare Bourbon, both former brands of Seagram. The recipe for whiskeys being made on contract agreements utilized Mash Bill #2, which report-edly was higher in rye content.

"Sometimes you've got to get lucky," said Goldring a few years ago in a Rouses blog interview, ". . .and you've got to be in the right place at the right time; and we bought the inventory, we got the distillery, and we started buying other brands from other major distillers." Blue chip brands, such as W.L. Weller and Old Charter, had become available due to the fact that many producers at that time were still wrestling with enormous expenses to hold inventories of unsold whiskey. Looking to the future, Sazerac purchased W.L. Weller and Old Charter from the new conglomer-ate on the international block, Diageo plc of London, England.

With his portfolio expanding, Goldring instructed master distiller Gary Gayheart to hire more production personnel. In 1994, Gayheart hired a young Kentuckian with two college degrees (chemical engineering and chemistry) by the name of Harlen Wheatley. Gayheart was hankering for retirement and was searching for a successor. "I wanted a long-term career," Wheatley told me in a 2020 interview. "It was November and Gary and I walked around the plant complex, which was eerily quiet. They weren't distilling that week. The bottling line was operating only two days a week. Things weren't as pretty as they are now so for me it was a big leap of faith . . . I kept thinking 'why do you need me?'"

Goldring next zeroed in on Mark Brown. Brown, who had earlier served within the Sazerac Company from 1981 to 1992 in various execu-tive roles such as director of new products, national sales manager, and vice president of marketing, was at the time in his fifth year of employ-ment at rival Brown-Forman. His role there was as COO of the company's Select Brands group. Five years after purchasing Buffalo Trace Distillery, Goldring enticed the respected industry executive to come back and lead Buffalo Trace. An MBA graduate of Tulane University in New Orleans, Brown accepted and was given the posts of both president and CEO, succeeding Peter Bordeaux, who had departed the company. And, with Brown in complete accord with Goldring, the search for the elusive Holy Grail of bourbon began in earnest.

Mark Brown was born in England. Brown has described his first five years, saying, "I grew up under a bar, figuratively and literally. My parents had a free house in [Dorking] England . . ." In case you are not aware of the term "free house," it means a public house (pub) or an inn in which the ownership offers a wide range of beers from multiple breweries, not just a single supplier. He immigrated to the state of Maryland to relaunch a once popular brand of British cider, H.P. Bulmer. But sales were sluggish, so after five years he started to work for Sazerac Company. "In those days, Sazerac was a regional company and only did business in nine states when I [first] joined. We had just 27 customers and 10 brands, so my role was primarily about opening up new markets the company had never been in."[10]

Upon his return to the Sazerac Company in 1997, he sensed a cautious and deflated feeling that appeared to emanate especially from the Frankfort distillery complex. "I recall walking around the plant, looking at the peeling paint on the buildings, the rusted barbed wire fencing, and thinking that this place needs a lot of beautifying. I admit that I did ask myself, 'What have I gotten into?'... Once the layers of paint were removed, the original beauty of the buildings was realized," Brown told me last year. He then began by unearthing the distillery's history. "The more we learned about the history and pedigree, the more fascinated and infatuated we became."

Clinging to the hope that the cyclicality of the marketplace for bourbon would swing back in a positive direction, Goldring and Brown instructed the Frankfort crew to begin major renovations and machinery upgrades. When, under Gary Gayheart's supervision, the comprehensive repair and makeover work was completed after two years, Goldring made the decision to give the distillery a new name, one that was befitting of its illustrious heritage and historically important location. Thus, Buffalo Trace Distillery was christened in homage to the place where, for centuries, gargantuan herds of buffalo splashed across the shoals of the Kentucky River, traveling west to the prairies that were lush in succulent grasses. In honor of the new distillery name, a new brand of bourbon was also created, Buffalo Trace Straight Kentucky Bourbon Whiskey.

With the rejuvenated distillery came a challenging directive, an edict from the top to master distiller Gary Gayheart: Make the finest bourbon America has ever tasted. Said Goldring in a 2016 interview, "You can't just go out and open a distillery, as it takes a long aging process to make a good bourbon. We are aging whiskey anywhere from three to 23 years, and there are dozens of formulas in the process. I am constantly looking for improvement in the product lines, never settling for anything less." With Goldring's sights set on creating a new standard of American whiskey, he admitted, "I'm in search of the Holy Grail." Goldring's desire to honor the pedigree of Buffalo Trace by blazing new pathways became an inter-company mission. From the original two mash bills, in 2021, Harlen Wheatley employs 11 distinct grain recipes.

Not long into his tenure, Brown met up with Ronnie Eddins, the plant's long-time warehouse manager. Brown listened as Eddins discussed the intricacies of barrel-aging, warehouse location, the subtle differences between barrel staves made from the tops and the bottoms of 80-year-old white oak trees, and how the fog that wafted off the neighboring Kentucky River affected the barrels. Brown was enthralled with Eddins's musings on what it might take to create the perfect bourbon.

Soon after that discussion, Buffalo Trace's relentless quest for the Holy Grail was launched.

The Sazerac Cocktail and Resurrection of Sazerac House

I can't think of any other cocktail, aside from the glorious Manhattan, that is so closely identified with a city as the Sazerac is with New Orleans. The book of Sazerac cocktail mythology ranks with the best in mixed drink and bar lore. This is a cocktail designed to be controversial, exotic, and alluring. It made a brief appearance in the 1973 James Bond film *Live and Let Die*, starring Roger Moore, when the storyline shifted to New Orleans.

Some Sazerac recipes call for bourbon as the base, others for rye, and still others suggest employing both whiskey and cognac as the foundational spirits. The inclusion of absinthe, which is legendary in its own right, in the majority of recipes adds to the mystique of this seductive cocktail. As for bitters, bartenders in New Orleans favor Peychaud's while bartenders elsewhere sometimes use Angostura. So which Sazerac cocktail recipe is the best? That determination I will leave to your own 10,000 taste buds. However, the one I prefer comes from the brilliant book *Cocktail Codex*:[a]

Ingredients:

Vieux Pontarlier Absinthe (with which to rinse the glass)

1.5 ounces Rittenhouse Rye Whiskey

0.5 ounce Pierre Ferrand 1840 Cognac

1 teaspoon Demerara Gum Syrup

4 dashes Peychaud's Bitters

1 dash Angostura Bitters

Garnish: lemon twist

Instructions:

First rinse a squat old-fashioned glass with the absinthe; dump. Stir the rye, cognac, Demerara Gum Syrup, and bitters over ice in shaker; strain into rinsed old-fashioned tumbler. Gently squeeze the lemon twist over the cocktail, throw the twist away. Cheers.

As for recent news concerning the Sazerac House, in December of 2016 Sazerac Company bought two buildings on the corner of Canal and Magazine streets. The prime location is just a few hundred feet from the original 1850 Sazerac Coffee-House site. On October 2, 2019, the newly constructed Sazerac House opened its doors. The three-floor, 48,000-square-feet exhibit space features an on-site distillery for the making of Sazerac Rye in a 500-gallon still, a bottling line, private events rooms, the Peychaud's Bitters production operation, and multiple exhibits that highlight the history of the first Sazerac House and the creation of cocktails, including the Sazerac Cocktail.

Note

a. Alex Day, Nick Fauchald, and David Kaplan. *Cocktail Codex: Fundamentals, Formulas, Evolutions*. New York: Ten Speed Press, 2018, p. 33.

15

"Experimentation Is in Our DNA . . ."

THE WHISKEYS FROM the leading quartet of whiskey producing nations, the United States, Scotland, Ireland, and Canada, largely remained unchanged in terms of flavor profiles and production modes until the final 15 years of the twentieth century. Mainstream whiskeys, such as Jack Daniel's Tennessee Sour Mash, Jim Beam Kentucky Straight Bourbon, Glenfiddich Pure Malt Scotch (as it was labeled at its launch in 1963), J & B Rare Blended Scotch, The Glenlivet 12-year-old Single Malt Scotch, and Dewar's White Label Blended Scotch, all tasted in 1985 much as they did in 1965. This industry-wide occurrence wasn't due as much to disinterest on the part of the distilleries as to complacency. "If it's working relatively well as is, why mess with it?" was the accepted *modus operandi.*

In addition, the American drinking public and bartenders of the postwar era, in particular, had come to rely on these brands without exercising the type of curiosity that abounds now in the first quarter of the twenty-first century. Consumers and drinking establishment servers in 1959 and

1972 weren't especially interested in the provenance or novelty of their favorite whiskey. They didn't give a particular hoot about what the grain recipe happened to be or in what type of barrel it had been stored or whether the warehouse had a concrete or a dirt floor. Their interest was confined within the psychological fences of how much a whiskey cost, what kind of buzz they or their customers would get, and whether or not it came in a large 1.75-liter jug. Therefore, with the demand for new and innovative concepts comparatively dormant, the whiskey distillers were satisfied with the perceived security of the status quo.

Unfortunately, not all brands flourished by playing the status quo card, as sales figures point out. Even throughout the "dark ages" endured by American whiskey distillers from the late 1960s to the late 1990s, major product makeovers and new brand introductions were few and far between, the exceptions being the aforementioned Blanton's Single Barrel, Wild Turkey Rare Breed, and Jim Beam's Small Batch Collection. And even those groundbreaking brands, as previously discussed, didn't initially fare well largely due to their lofty price tags.

What can be determined by this general trade-wide lack of innovation is that the new introductions that had been offered had failed to capture an appreciable share of the general audience. Remember the miserable public reception that welcomed "light whiskeys" covered in Chapter 13? In Elmer T. Lee's daily journals he openly discussed how hard it was to convince consumers at tasting events in the late 1980s and 1990s to try and then purchase a new bourbon brand like Blanton's Single Barrel, which was priced at $35, when they were used to buying a popular favorite such as Old Crow from $6 to $8. Trial and error in brand creation usually resulted in error and, by extension, the hellish nightmares suffered by industry executives forced to face the unpleasant music orchestrated by their superiors when they were asked for an accounting. So the whiskey industry, in particular the one centered in the American heartland, stagnated out of over-caution, the meteoric ascension of vodka, and the abject terror of public failure and ridicule. All of which makes Elmer T. Lee's gutsy decision to launch Blanton's Single Barrel Bourbon in what was an arid wasteland of ideas seem all the more intrepid.

Yet as has been presented in earlier chapters, the historical data depict that there had existed a keen sense of experimentation and daring throughout the lineage of Buffalo Trace distillers and owners. From E.H. Taylor, Jr.'s relentless, uncompromising pursuit of making the best nineteenth century Kentucky whiskey in copper equipment to George T. Stagg's installation of steam heating in warehouses in 1886 and the building of a new high-volume distillery, the Carlisle, to Albert Blanton carrying out Lewis Rosenstiel's stern directives to maintain the highest production standards in the post-Prohibition years to Elmer T. Lee's game-changing epiphany, the distillers at the Leestown site had as the record shows chased excellence and distinction through innovation since 1870.

Kris Comstock was the Buffalo Trace Distillery senior marketing director when I interviewed him in late 2020. Kris departed in January 2021, but his insights still ring true. Having worked at BTD since January of 2003 strictly on the marketing side, Comstock had his finger on the company pulse. He succinctly summarized this company desire to always push the envelope, saying, "Experimentation is in our DNA. It's been there since E.H. Taylor and his pursuit for excellence . . . True, we're a big distillery but within this complex we're also a craft distillery that experiments." Concurred current master distiller Harlen Wheatley, who assumed that role after Gary Gayheart's retirement in 2005, "We're carrying the torch that E.H. Taylor lit in the 1870s, no doubt."

A superb example of an employee who embodied the commitment to being bold and venturesome was the late warehouse manager Ronnie Eddins, a contemporary of Elmer T. Lee. Eddins was hired in 1961. After initially working on the bottling line and in the shipping department for several years, he was assigned to warehouse operations. In 1984, the year of Blanton's Single Barrel release, Eddins was named to one of the more inconspicuous but vital distillery jobs, that of Warehouse Manager. Working in tandem with his friend and colleague, Leonard Riddle, Eddins became a respected authority on such issues as the best way to inspect new barrel stave deliveries, properly filling the barrels with whiskey, laboriously hunting down leaking barrels in the warehouses and then patching them up, determining the optimal warehouse placement for the newly filled barrels, and understanding the seasonal temperature variations of each of the company's roster of 13 warehouses. Eddins's position demanded that he master these tasks in order to closely monitor the aging cycle of every barrel, all 300,000 of them. Rarely does someone come along with the acumen and uncanny insight of a Ronnie Eddins.

But Eddins's story is one about pure curiosity, an unbridled inquisitiveness that mushroomed into something spectacular. As part of his job, Eddins traveled to the Independent Stave Company in the Missouri Ozarks region to examine and choose white oak trees for use as barrels. One could say that Eddins was that rare individual who could clearly see the forest for the trees. On one particular trip in the late 1990s he selected 96 old white oak trees for a specific undertaking that would eventually be dubbed the Single Oak Project (SOP). Eddins, with the blessing of new CEO Mark Brown, had a quest, a personal mission to try to find the right combination of key factors with which to make the ideal bourbon. The baseline of the experiment would be the 192 barrels, gleaned from the top and bottom halves of the 96 trees. Eddins' idea, in conjunction with the distilling team, was to ascertain how 192 bourbons would react in 192 individual barrels, with each barrel's maturation being guided by a unique set of conditions based upon seven variables. Could the Holy Grail of bourbons be identified using these criteria?

The seven factors that would come after eight years of barrel aging to produce 192 distinctive experimental bourbons were:

1. *Mash bill:* the recipe consisting of either a corn-WHEAT-barley or corn-RYE-barley combination

2. *Variety of warehouse:* a wooden rick floor or a concrete floor

3. *Length of barrel stave seasoning:* oak staves left either 6 or 12 months in open air and elements so that natural impurities can be leeched out

4. *Char level of the oak barrels:* level three or the deeper level four – bourbon by definition must be aged in new oak barrels that have been fire-charred on the inside to varying degrees, defined as being on a scale of level one, the lightest, to level four, the most heavily charred

5. *Top or bottom half of oak tree:* each tree provided only one barrel from each end

6. *Grain of the tree:* designated as tight grain, average grain, or coarse grain – the grain type involves cell size, surface appearance, degree of porosity, and direction of the wood cells

7. *Entry proof:* degree of alcohol percentage of the whiskey when it is pumped into the oak barrel, either 105-proof/52.5% alcohol or 125-proof/62.5% alcohol

The concept, as well as the actual preparation for the 192 barrels, was mind-bogglingly complex. Veteran whiskey journalist Liza Weisstuch, who participated as a taster in the project, called the SOP, ". . . the human genome project of the spirits world. Just think of the sheer mindboggling mathematics of it all. Only Buffalo Trace would take on such an epic project in order to learn more about the production process."

For easier understanding of the intricacies of the project that was undertaken by Eddins and the Buffalo Trace team, I offer the following two paragraphs as, hopefully, illustrations of the scope of the SOP and what it proposed to determine:

A) Under the guidelines of the SOP, Whiskey #1 would have a factor list that would include having corn-wheat-barley recipe, a barrel taken from the top of a white oak with tight-grained staves that were seasoned outdoors for six months, then charred to level three. The whiskey would be pumped into the barrel at 105-proof and the barrel would be stored in a warehouse with a concrete floor.

B) Whiskey #2, again purely for example's sake, would purposely share all the same variables of #1 except for one, the mash bill recipe, which would instead be corn-rye-barley rather than number one's corn-wheat-barley. With six of the deciding factors between #1 and #2 identical, tasters, both professionals and average consumers, were charged with the task of discerning which recipe was preferred and, more importantly, why.

For the purpose of obtaining as much professional and private data as possible, when the whiskeys were deemed ready to disperse Mark Brown decided to open up the SOP to acknowledged whiskey journalists (including yours truly, spirits critic Christopher Null, the aforementioned Liza Weisstuch, Lew Bryson, Chuck Cowdery, and others) as well as to any consumers who expressed an interest in participating. Liquor stores also became involved acting as conduits between Buffalo Trace and consumers. Over a four-year span, the journalists and consumers took part in this intriguing exercise, answering a questionnaire that featured a dozen questions that arrived with each of the 16 sets containing 12 individual bourbons. The distillery reported that, "In total, 5,645 people participated in the Single Oak Project which collected 5,086 unique whiskey reviews. On average, each of the 192 whiskies was evaluated 26.2 times."

Aside from being a clever public relations coup for the distillery, the Single Oak Project served to provide exceptionally detailed information about what types of bourbon could be produced in the future using different criteria. The most highly regarded bottling of the 192 proved to be SOP #80, a luscious bourbon with a heavy rye percentage that was matured in a level-four char barrel from the bottom half of a white oak tree with average grain. The staves were air-dried for 12 months in the open air and the entry proof was 125. The barrel was stored in a concrete floor warehouse for eight years.

But, was the accumulated data worth the herculean effort? "The knowledge gained from conducting this research experiment is priceless," concluded Mark Brown. "We can now compare and confirm how each of these variables in the bourbon-making process affects the finished product, which will only assist our experimental program and help us create even better whiskeys in the future."

Could the SOP barrel #80 be bourbon's Holy Grail? In the view of some whiskey lovers, perhaps it can be. The winning formula has been reproduced and is currently aging in Frankfort. The projected release date is 2025. What is so undeniably compelling boils down to the unbridled spirit of adventure that permeates the Buffalo Trace Distillery team. Predictably, there have been some muttered concerns by intramural rivals that Buffalo Trace's mission to push boundaries might be as much P.T. Barnum as genuine scientific interest. One thing is certain, however: Many people who are making American whiskey follow Buffalo Trace's exploratory excursions more than for the fun of it.

"Bubble, bubble, toil and trouble"

As if the SOP didn't keep the distilling and wood-aging teams in Frankfort occupied enough in the early 2000s, there is Buffalo Trace's equally quirky Experimental Collection program, which debuted in 2006. These limited edition, one-barrel-only whiskeys are drawn in small lots from 25,000 barrels of whiskey that are considered as purely experimental and are housed within the company's network of 26 warehouses that overall currently shelter 1.1 million barrels. Seventeen warehouses are located directly on the main campus grounds and nine are situated on the company-owned farm nestled next to the main complex.

The 375-milliliter bottles of the Experimental Collection cost $46.99 each and are in painfully minute quantities for consumers due to the diminutive size of the experiments. This collection includes off-the-charts experiments on barrels that have been toasted and charred in varying degrees of intensity to ascertain the effects of the burnt oak on whiskey, the employment of different types of grain combinations in the mash bills, like those involving rarely used grains such as oats and rice, and the use of unusual types of wood for the late stages of the maturation process, including the use of wine barrels that previously housed zinfandel and chardonnay.

To give a glimpse at a recent example of this program that came out in April of 2020, the 23rd such release, the premise focused on the importance of water, according to master distiller Harlen Wheatley. This individual whiskey employed a bourbon recipe that included wheat, along with corn and barley. The whiskey was pumped into a new barrel on December 10, 2007, at 114-proof (57 percent alcohol) in Warehouse C and allowed to rest for four years. It was then pulled from the barrel, reduced with water to 100-proof (50 percent alcohol), pumped back into the same barrel and left to mature in the same warehouse for eight additional years. Said Wheatley of the experiment's purpose, "We've always known water was a necessary component in making whiskey. This experiment helped us to understand how important a role water actually plays . . . The result of this experiment led us to a bourbon that is actually one of my favorite experiments."[1]

Another of the distillery's experimental endeavors into the unknown is the Single Estate project. This fully agricultural undertaking utilizes 282 acres of nearby land to cultivate different strains of heirloom corn, such as Boone County White corn, which dates back to 1876; Japonica Striped corn, a purple kernel variety from the 1890s; Neon Pink Popcorn; Royal Blue; Hickory Cane White; and CF790 Conventional corn. In the autumn of 2020, an ancient strain, simply called Indian Corn, dating from 1000 BCE was harvested with middling results. The concept here is to determine how varying strains of corn that are different from the most widely employed strain, the hybrid called Yellow Dent, will fare in the production of bourbon. Since by law any straight bourbon's makeup must contain a minimum of 51 percent corn, the outcome of this project potentially may affect the future of bourbon production in terms of the most critical base material. Every harvested crop is distilled and rested in barrels on site with the eventual purpose of becoming a new line of whiskeys termed the Single Estate collection.

Then, in the continuing saga of Buffalo Trace's search for bourbon's Holy Grail, there is Warehouse X, a relatively small building tucked inconspicuously into Buffalo Trace's maze-like industrial complex. Warehouse X's experiments examine the impact of environment on the aging process. Built in four distinct, hall-like chambers, experiments have been afoot since 2014 that include the measuring of humidity levels, airflow currents, sunlight, and temperature and their collective and individual effects on barrels of whiskey and their contents. After the first three years of operation, no less than 3.5 million data points had been collected. As of October of 2020, the single experiment that registered how changes in temperature influence a whiskey's maturation patterns had alone yielded 1.3 million points of data.

Harlen Wheatley described Warehouse X's purpose in a 2017 interview with writer Tim Knittel of DistillerBlog,[2] saying, "The Warehouse X project – we called it 'The Future of Aging'. So for us it's about how we treat our barrels in the future, to make plans for the future, based on these results, which unfortunately will take 20 years to get what we need."

An entire battery of calibrations are taken regularly in Warehouse X, including monthly quantifications like lumen readings to monitoring

Present day Master Distiller Harlen Wheatley

sunlight levels in each chamber, temperature, airflow, humidity, and psi pressure, meaning the units of pressure expressed in pounds of force per square inch in a prescribed area. The information gathered down the road from the Warehouse X exercises will likely dictate how new warehouses should be constructed and possibly how established warehouse space can be refitted to gain the maximum advantages from the temperate north-central Kentucky environment.

Acknowledging that the commitment to innovation, revolution, and restless transformation that permeates the Buffalo Trace culture can be viewed from the outside with admiration, as well as you-must-be-kidding skepticism, master distiller Harlen Wheatley reacted by saying in 2020, "Our motto is 'Embrace Change.' Embracing change means not resting on our laurels." The distillery's quartet of major experimental projects, the Single Oak Project, the Single Estate program, the Experimental Collection, and Warehouse X, could not be conceived of and then carried out by a company that didn't have deep resources and an equally fathomless ocean of resolve that starts at the top level of management.

Wheatley summarizes his vision on three of his pet projects like this, "Warehouse X is focused on the environment. Single Oak is focused on the trees, how they are turned into wood, which in turn are turned into the barrel, so we focused on the tree. The [Single] Estate is focused on the grain, a little bit on the soil, but mainly on the grain . . . Warehouse X is probably a minimum of 20 years. The Estate program is probably forever, there's no end to that one. And Single Oak was kinda finite . . ." Pondering the sheer logistical complications posed by the SOP, Wheatley laughed. "It was kind of a nightmare . . ." But such can be the price of derring-do.

Are Buffalo Trace's expensive to operate experimental programs going to continue past the four monster experiments, three of which are still in motion? All indications from the key executives involved point to an affirmative response.

What's been learned thus far? Wheatley responds. "We've learned a ton about warehouses and the importance of their environments, the effects of temperature and humidity, about barrels, about warehouse location. Especially since we are now building more warehouses, we're utilizing information about insulation, sunlight, the type of flooring, and airflow. Warehouse X has also provided numerous data that allow us to prepare for the taste profiles that we want. It all goes toward the consistency of our whiskeys . . . I think that the line of whiskeys that most reflects what we're learning from the six years of experiments [in Warehouse X] currently is our expanding E.H. Taylor lineup of whiskeys."

The intense drive for change at Buffalo Trace could, in part, be attributed to Elmer T. Lee's decision to release Blanton's way back in 1984. "Single barrel" wasn't even a term until Lee coined it. Just as strong a case could also be made that the pedigree of distillers and owners beginning with E.H. Taylor, Jr. instilled a sense of restless pursuit.

"Let's face it, [the Single Oak Project] was somewhat crazy," admits public relations director Amy Preske. "From the public relations side, it's hard to sell that story because it's so complex, so geeky, but the good news comes from what we learned from it. Here, Ronnie Eddins had begun his experiments before Mark Brown arrived in 1997. It had to take a huge leap of faith from Ronnie's side to tell Mark, his new boss, about what he was doing on his own time. And Mark, to his credit, listened and was fascinated . . . so doubtless it starts at the top of the pyramid. Everyone [at Buffalo Trace] buys into the vision of Mark, who is never satisfied. It's the leadership that pushes everyone forward."

16

"Resistance Is Futile"

ACQUISITION HAS BEEN as much a key element of the recent Sazerac/
Buffalo Trace success story as have been its rosters of stimulating and inventive personalities and fabled American whiskey brands. But while brand
and company ownership swapping enjoys a long tradition in the beverage
alcohol trade, Sazerac's version of absorbing brands whose germination
occurred in the laboratories and distilleries of other beverage companies is
unparalleled in its scope. When one views the astonishing record of brand
and company purchases made by the Sazerac Company since 1989, the
famous line of the villainous Borg entity from the *Star Trek: The Next Generation* late 1980s television series comes to mind: "Resistance is futile."
In 2021, Sazerac Company's portfolio includes no less than 450 brands, a
good number of which are of the value-level, inexpensive variety that rakes
in substantial gross revenues from their volume. To sustain the inventory
turnover in case depletions across its portfolio, the Sazerac Empire squires
over seven distillery complexes and employs 2,600 women and men.

But, do the hundreds of lower-priced brands in all categories fly in the
face of Sazerac's cultivated image of prestige, heritage, and top quality? As
explained by CEO and president Mark Brown on the purpose of owning

scores of lower- and middle-range brands to me in the autumn of 2020, "We believe that consumers at all levels should have the freedom to select from a variety of quality choices in their spirits purchases. The majority of consumers cannot afford to buy, much less locate, a Pappy Van Winkle or a Blanton's whiskey. That segment of the buying public is every bit as important to us as the smaller, more affluent group with deeper pockets. Ours is proudly a democratic approach to marketing all these hundreds of products. It's our company mission then to make certain that our lower-priced brands, take Benchmark [bourbon], for example, display as much quality and craftsmanship as the more expensive bourbon brands."

This company philosophy of offering a broad range of products at every price level is hardly virgin territory when one examines the history of the large, influential beverage companies of the past century. In the post-Prohibition period, Joseph E. Seagram & Sons, Hiram Walker & Sons, National Distillers, and indeed the one-time twentieth-century owner of the George T. Stagg Distillery, Schenley, each boasted lengthy and varied brand portfolios. Contemporary beverage international giants, like Pernod Ricard (nearly 60 spirits and wine brands), Diageo plc. (200+), Brown-Forman (25), Heaven Hill Distilleries (almost 50), Gruppo Campari (50+), Bacardi Limited (200+), Constellation Brands (100+), Beam Suntory (60+), E&J Gallo (100+), and more, operate by this playbook. This pyramid approach of value products providing the base for the more elite products is a tried and true business model honed after the repeal of Prohibition in 1933. This archetype is how the major mainstream beverage companies maintain their far-reaching status, year after year, while absorbing occasional marketplace turbulence.

Buy, Buy, Buy!

The following is an abbreviated account of Sazerac's breathtaking number of transactions involving the purchasing of beverage alcohol firms, of distilleries, and of individual brands since 1989, some of which were later either discontinued or sold off, though most have been retained and are available today.

Year 1989: As previously cited, from Joseph E. Seagram came Benchmark Bourbon, Eagle Rare Bourbon, James Foxe Canadian Whisky, Nikolai Vodka, Carstairs Blended Whiskey, Crown Russe Vodka and Gin, and Dr. McGillicuddy's liqueurs, the most important expression of which was Fireball Whisky, which later morphed into the riotously popular, 5.65 million-case-per-year (in 2019)[1] cash-cow known by hundreds of thousands of college students from northern Maine to southern California as Fireball Cinnamon Whisky.

1992: As previously cited, the procuring from Japanese beverage firm Takara Shuzo Company, Ltd., of the George T. Stagg whiskey inventory along with the Stagg distillery (Frankfort, Kentucky), though Takara Shuzo remained (and still remains) the brand owner of Blanton's Single Barrel Kentucky Straight Bourbon.

1994: Monsieur Henri, a wine and spirits purveyor, later to become Gemini Spirits and Wine, whose portfolio has at various times consisted of Siete Leguas Tequila, Del Maguey Single Village Mezcal, Banks Rum, Glenfarclas Single Malt Scotch, Campo de Encanto Pisco, Casa San Matias Tequila, Dimmi Liquore di Milano.

1999: The absorption of the iconic W. L. Weller and Old Charter (brand slogan: *The whiskey that never watches the clock*) bourbon whiskey brands from Diageo, plc. (London, England).

2003: Buys the A. Smith Bowman Distillery (Fredericksburg, Virginia), which was established in 1934 and shipped its first whiskey in 1937.

2009: Acquires spirits brands from Constellation Brands (Victor, New York), including Barton Brands and the Barton 1792 Distillery (Bardstown, Kentucky), founded in 1879, plus warehouses and a bottling plant/distillery (Glemore) in Owensburg, Kentucky, for $334 million; the purchase of the Old Taylor Bourbon label, barrel inventory from Beam Global Spirits & Wine (today's Beam Suntory, Chicago, Illinois).

2011: Bought for $32.9 million from Corby Distilleries Limited of Windsor, Ontario, Canada (today's Corby Spirit and Wine Limited),

Red Tassel Vodka, DeKuyper Geneva Gin and Peachtree Schnapps plus 14 more brands; this agreement included shares of Corby's plants in Montreal, Quebec, Canada, most prominently, later to be renamed Old Montreal Distillery. A busy year, 2011, as Sazerac also purchases 32 brands from White Rock Distillery (Lewiston, Maine).

2012: White Rock Distillery (Lewiston, Maine) sells more brands to Sazerac Company; Sazerac also acquires Gran Gala Liqueur from Stock Spirits.

2013: Buys distillery, property, and all equipment in Lewiston, Maine (formerly White Rock), from Beam, Inc. (today's Beam Suntory); title of Lewiston distillery complex changed to Boston Brands of Maine in 2017.

2015: Acquires the Irish whiskey brand Michael Collins from Eagle Sellers' Rep, LLC; integrates Van Gogh Imports (New York, New York), changing the name to 375 Park Avenue Spirits.

2016: Purchases from Brown-Forman, Inc. (Louisville, Kentucky) Southern Comfort and Tuaca Liqueur for $543.5 million; buys the Irish whiskey brand Paddy from the Pernod Ricard company Irish Distillers (County Cork, Ireland); acquires the top-shelf specialty spirits company specializing in bottling very old spirits, The Last Drop Distillers (London, England); buys Pinnacle Drinks from South Trade International of Australia; purchases The Popcorn Sutton Distillery (Newport, Tennessee); snatches up Fris Vodka from Pernod Ricard; and buys Domaine Breuil de Segonzac (Cognac, Segonzac, France).

2018: For $550 million, Sazerac purchases 19 inexpensive brands, including Seagram VO Canadian Whisky, Romana Sambuca, Scoresby and John Begg blended Scotch whiskies, Parrot Bay (rum), Yukon Jack Liqueur, Popov Vodka, Myers's Rum, Goldschlager schnapps and more from Diageo, plc (London, England).

2019: From Star Industries and Black Prince Distillery (Clifton, New Jersey), Sazerac buys 19 low-end brands that include Georgi, Alexi, and Majorska vodkas, Blansac Brandy, Carnaby's Gin, Clyde's Gin, Dorada Tequila, McColl's Blended Scotch whisky, R. J. Hodges Bourbon, Devil Springs Vodka, Black Prince Scotch, and more.

CEO and President Mark Brown

2020: Buys the 160-year-old bourbon brand Early Times, as well as Canadian Mist, Collingwood from Brown-Forman (Louisville, Kentucky), a deal that included the Canadian Mist Distillery; purchases Paul Masson Brandy from Constellation Brands (Victor, New York) for $255 million.

"I'm always looking for more brands to acquire," said Mark Brown to me last autumn. "I see no end to it as long as the new products make sense for our greater portfolio. If it provides a good fit and is in line with our philosophy and we can afford it, I will buy it or come to a partnership agreement."

In 2016, there was one particular buyout that deserves a deeper in-depth look because it speaks volumes about the Sazerac Company doctrine and business strategy.

Good to The Last Drop

The First Industrial Revolution mushroomed in continental Europe, the British Isles, and North America between the years of 1760 to 1840, introducing the concept of the mass manufacturing of common goods and merchandise that would become widely available at all levels of society. Since that era, each major international industry has boasted its own cadre of legendary figures, the women and men who through innovation and insight have altered the course of that trade sector for the better. The beverage alcohol industry in the twentieth century had a lion's share of inventive individuals whose original thinking broke new ground. Two of those giants that hailed from the British Isles were the late Tom Jago and James Espey, OBE (Officer of the Order of the British Empire). Between Jago and Espey, they created an impressive list of successful beverage alcohol products that in some cases redefined a whole spirits category and in others created a new category altogether.

Their landmark creations included The Classic Malts of Scotland, launched in 1988 under Espey's guidance, which did more than any other marketing concept to promote Scotland's whisky regions through six definitive single malt whiskies; Bailey's Irish Cream, a product developed by Tom Jago that upon its release in 1974 created a new liqueur category that is popular to this day; Johnnie Walker Blue Label, a James Espey creation, was the initial luxury blended Scotch that debuted in 1992 and for its first decade and a half was the Pappy Van Winkle of its time; Malibu, a low-alcohol coconut-flavored rum, was introduced by Jago in 1982 and has continued to be a staple product of any liquor store's inventory, now for Pernod Ricard; and Chivas Regal 18, launched in 1997 by Espey and blended by master blender Colin Scott, is the equal of many and the better of some single malt Scotches.[2]

In 2007, the retired Espey had a revelation while on holiday at a boutique hotel in South Africa, called the Last Word. Feeling that in the new century beverage alcohol product innovation had gone the way of SONY Walkmans, Espey's mind flashed on the small lots of whisky he knew were collecting dust in Scotland's warehouses that would never see the light of day because of their advanced age. Once back in London, he phoned his old friend, the retired Tom Jago, and told him, "We've got one last challenge."[3] They, along with Peter Fleck, decided in 2008 to open The Last Drop Distillers, Ltd.

Once the legalities were resolved, the search was on for old and forgotten Scotch whiskies. Said Espey, "Tom found this incredible blend of old whiskies, the youngest of which was 1960 . . . It was like nectar; old but fresh . . ."[4] As time and market victories followed, the Last Drop line expanded to include mature cognacs and armagnacs, bourbons, and even ancient ports. While James Espey took to the road to promote The Last Drop, his daughter, Beanie, and Tom Jago's daughter, Rebecca, took the reins of day-to-day company management.

Admitted Espey of the enterprise, "I saw myself as an entrepreneur and as an incubator for the brand because it needed a parent of size . . . I saw The Last Drop as a vehicle for the future, as the world's most exclusive spirits collection. I didn't have the money to finance a lot of stock and I always intended to sell it."[5] Conversations about a possible sale were held with Diageo plc in London and Pernod Ricard in Paris in 2014–2015, but turned out fruitless. Then in 2016, they received an offer from Mark Brown. The headline in *The Spirits Business* on September 6, 2016, splashed across the Internet, "The Sazerac Company has acquired The Last Drop Distillers Limited, a British family-run spirits bottler, for an undisclosed sum." In Espey's view, this was an inevitable happening. Declared Espey, "This acquisition marks the next stage of The Last Drop Distillers story that will see us take the brand to the next level while retaining and building our core values of exclusivity, craft, and excellence."

Managing director Rebecca Jago told me in the fall of 2020, "Had the business landed in the hands of a huge multinational company such as Diageo or Pernod Ricard we all just would have walked away with a check in hand but with nothing left to do. In those scenarios The Last Drop would have been placed at the mercy of a brand manager and the company accountants. Not a good place to be for a project like The Last Drop, which requires imagination as much as it does dedication. With Sazerac and Mark Brown, we're [Jago and Beanie Geraedts-Espey] still deeply engaged with the decisions and direction of the company. He [Brown] has a natural feel for when to allow people to be their creative best. Basically he just told us to keep on running it as we were and to continue to find new treasures."

The commitment by Sazerac Company to The Last Drop appears to be of the "all in" variety, even including warehouse experiments. Said Jago in an interview in December 2019, "We are in the middle of conducting a groundbreaking experiment in the Warehouse P wing of Buffalo Trace Distillery in Kentucky, aging a number of bourbon barrels in a carefully controlled environment to mimic the temperatures of Scotland. Some barrels will be left untouched but closely monitored for up to 50 years. Despite the lack of ability to forecast the market decades into the future, this experiment facilitates building on The Last Drop legacy."[6] Mark Brown, ever enthusiastic, was delighted with the purchase, saying at the conclusion of the deal, "As a family-owned company we fully appreciate the value of a small, engaged, and passionate team in a venture such as The Last Drop Distillers and look forward to continuing the excellent progress the business has made since its inception."[7]

In late October of 2020, Buffalo Trace released the inaugural fall Last Drop Distillers collection. The three-bottle set consisted of an old bourbon whiskey distilled in 1980 at what was then the George T. Stagg Distillery, a 33-year-old over-proof Jamaican rum (67.9% alcohol), and a vintage Grande Champagne cognac distilled in 1959. They were not cheap, mind you, so before you reach for the checkbook, pause for a moment. Respectively, their suggested retail prices were listed as $4,600, $3,400, and $5,200 per bottle. After all, The Last Drop, in this case, really means just that.

Pappy: The One, the Only

In the 2000s, in addition to the dizzying array of purchases already outlined, William Goldring also entered Sazerac Company into a series of enterprising joint ventures, most of which have gone largely unnoticed while some have reaped enormous public relations and media coverage benefits. These partnerships, import, and distribution agreements have included an armagnac brand (Saint-Vivant), a New Orleans–based bitters concern (Bittermens), a Colombian rum (Dictador), Scandinavian aquavit brands (Lysholm Linie, Aalborg), and more.

But the single joint venture that garnered Sazerac and by direct extension Buffalo Trace Distillery the most print, electronic, and social media publicity, certainly in the whiskey arena, was the astute agreement made in 2002 with the Van Winkle family. That alliance stipulated that the Van Winkle line of soft-as-crushed-velvet "wheated" bourbons would be produced at the Buffalo Trace plant under the direct supervision of Julian Van Winkle III, the grandson of the legendary cigar-chomping whiskey salesman and brand owner Julian Prentice "Pappy" Van Winkle, who was born in Danville, Kentucky, in 1874. Further, and even better, from Van Winkle's perspective, Buffalo Trace would manage the distribution of the Pappy line of whiskeys through its vast network.

Though never a distiller himself, Pappy Van Winkle was a gifted marketer and traveling salesman, who began his career in 1935 at W.L. Weller and Son's wholesale business in Louisville, Kentucky. Soon he became a co-owner, along with his wholesale business partner Alex Farnsley and Arthur Phillip Stitzel, of the Stitzel-Weller Distillery, located in Shively, a nearby suburb of Louisville, Kentucky. That distillery produced such memorable bourbon brands as Old Fitzgerald, Rebel Yell, Cabin Still, Mammoth Cave, Belle of Bourbon, Old Elk, Old Weller, and Old Rip Van Winkle. The distillery's owners made much of the fact that they offered bourbon whiskeys made from a recipe that employed wheat in the mash bill instead of rye, which was the prevailing style of the era. "Wheated" bourbons (known today by the unfortunate moniker "wheaters"), they claimed, produced silky bourbons that were less aggressive than rye bourbons. A print advertisement from the post-Prohibition years touted seven-year-old Old Weller's ". . . Whisper of Wheat . . . the century-old secret that *flavor-softens* Mr. Weller's wonderful Bourbon!"

Pappy Van Winkle remained in charge of the brand until he died at the age of 91 in February of 1965. Following Van Winkle's death, his son Julian took the helm of the Stitzel-Weller Distillery, but after a few short years was placed in the regrettable position of having to unload the distillery due to the financial concerns of the stockholders and his family. Bourbon sales were flattening at that time and the prospects for growth were not encouraging. In June of 1972, the New York–based firm of industrialist Norton Simon, whose interests included a wide array of consumer products, bought the brand rights, then changed the distillery name to Old Fitzgerald Distillery after what they believed to be the flagship brand. United Distillers eventually became the proprietor and reestablished the distillery name of Stitzel-Weller. They shut down distillery operations in early 1992. In time, the Sazerac Company bought the rights to the Weller brand.

Meanwhile, Julian Van Winkle II formed a new company based upon the brand of Old Rip Van Winkle, which had been retained after the sale of his father's company to Norton Simon.[8] The company motto remained: "We make fine bourbon at a profit if we can, at a loss if we must, but always fine bourbon." Following Julian Van Winkle II's death, his son, third-generation Julian Van Winkle III, assumed the brand's leadership role. With his own son, JVW III currently keeps Pappy's four-generation vision alive. "These last few years of witnessing the brand's explosive growth have been the experience of a lifetime," expressed Julian Van Winkle III in my 2020 interview with him. "I wish that my grandfather and father would have lived to see the gains we've made."

The teaming of Buffalo Trace Distillery and the Old Rip Van Winkle brand over time triggered an unprecedented cascade of marketplace commotion that had never been seen before in the annals of modern American whiskey history. Beginning toward the end of the first decade of the twenty-first century, that affiliation made the term "Pappy" a clarion call, a kind of mesmerizing mantra for the most ardent of American whiskey devotees and collectors. The consumer frenzy developed from a perfect confluence of occurrences that included the minuscule quantities of the Van Winkle whiskeys (currently in the neighborhood of 7,000 cases/84,000 bottles annually), the lofty suggested prices, the folklore that surrounded Pappy Van Winkle, word of mouth, and the quality and unusually extended maturity of the whiskeys themselves.

Of course, this being the era of 24/7/365 news cycles and thus the accompanying mass hysteria, media features fueled the raging fire with provocative headlines, such as "The Insatiable Demand behind Pappy Van Winkle" in the May 24, 2017, edition of *Department 26/Strategic Intelligence*, or the NBC News feature from October 15, 2016, that was titled, "The Bourbon So Exclusive That Even Billionaires Can't Buy It," or *THRILLIST*'s August 23, 2017, story called "Pappy Van Winkle: When Bourbon Becomes a Status Symbol," to cite just a few of the tens of articles and headlines.

But beyond any doubt, one of the zaniest episodes involving Old Rip Van Winkle whiskeys, which as one could surmise won truckloads of over-heated media coverage, had to be "Pappygate." Gilbert "Toby" Curtsinger worked on the loading docks on Buffalo Trace campus. In 2015, police learned that Curtsinger and nine other people were involved in a stolen bourbon and steroid ring. The heisted whiskeys included cases of high-end Old Rip Van Winkle and Wild Turkey bourbons. The main perpe-trator, Curtsinger, boosted the cases, packed them in his pick-up truck, and concealed them beneath a tarp, all of which brought into question the issue of plant security. Following his arrest and faced with a menu of felony charges, Curtsinger pled "guilty" and in 2018 received a 15-year prison sentence. As an article in *Grub Street* from June 1, 2018, summed up in a tone of black humor, "On the bright side, the bourbon that begins being aged this year will probably be *really* good in 2033 when Curtsinger's sentence is up." But here is the final irony, the garnish if you will, of the bizarre Pappygate case. As reported by the *Louisville Courier Journal* newspaper on June 29, 2018, just 30 days into Curtsinger's 15-year sen-tence, Franklin County Circuit Judge Thomas Dawson Wingate ordered that Curtsinger be released from prison as a stiff lesson in "shock proba-tion." Mercy me.

The Van Winkle portfolio in 2020 comprised six expressions: Old Rip Van Winkle 10-Year-Old Handmade Bourbon, Old Rip Van Winkle 10-Year-Old Special Reserve Bourbon, Old Rip Van Winkle 13-Year-Old Family Reserve Rye, Pappy Van Winkle's Family Reserve 15-Year-Old Bourbon, Pappy Van Winkle's Family Reserve 20-Year-Old Bourbon, and Pappy Van Winkle's Family Reserve 23-Year-Old Bourbon. Their sug-gested prices, which of course amidst the annual late-year frenzy never reflect the extortionate market prices that run into the thousands of dol-lars, ran from $70 to $300. Whether deserved or not, the older Van Win-kles now routinely fetch four- and even five-digit prices.

Said Mark Brown to me in October of 2020 about Pappy Van Winkle, "It [Pappy Van Winkle] is a wonderful member of our portfolio, make no mistake, but it likewise is the most frustrating one because there is so lit-tle of it. How much could there be of 23-year-old bourbon? Not much. And yet some consumers have a difficult time comprehending that these bourbons that require time are indeed finite, and also that once that aging period is deemed to be over, that what's left in the barrel can be very little. Evaporation steals a lot of it."

Brown, who commendably replies personally to queries from the public, often has to field scores of incredulous requests concerning Pappy Van Winkle releases. Like the entreaty from the delusional person who was frustrated having a low placement on the waiting list for a new ultra-expensive Lamborghini motorcar. They had the temerity to ask Brown for a case of Pappy with which to bribe the car dealer so that they could leapfrog to a higher place in the queue. On the other side of the entreaty coin for Pappy, terminally ill people who have developed a burning desire for a bucket-list taste of America's most fabled bourbon have approached Brown for a bottle. "Of course," remarked Brown with no hint of exasperation, "those we check out before we act."

Basking in the "Halo" of the BTAC

Without a doubt, the whiskeys that provide the most radiant "halo" effect for the entire Buffalo Trace Distillery whiskey portfolio is the assemblage of two straight ryes and three straight bourbons that comprise the annual limited edition offering known as the Buffalo Trace Antique Collection (BTAC). The three straight bourbons – George T. Stagg uncut/unfiltered/barrel strength, Eagle Rare 17-Year-Old, and William Larue Weller uncut/unfiltered/barrel strength – and the two straight ryes – Thomas H. Handy Sazerac Rye uncut/unfiltered/barrel strength and Sazerac 18-Year-Old Rye – have since 2006 headlined this yearly autumn release. In 2020, the suggested retail price of each whiskey was $99.99. Like the Van Winkles, however, the street prices can reach into the thousands of dollars per bottle due to the scarcity factor.

Because of the small quantities, each BTAC is eked out seemingly through an eyedropper in painfully minute amounts that are released in allotments to key whiskey retailers across the nation, as once again the annual amount of each whiskey is determined solely by its advanced age. Following the release of the BTAC each fall, the resultant reactions predictably unfold in four stages. First is the initial *outrage stage* that no one ever gets enough to satisfy them and why doesn't Buffalo Trace just make more; second is the *deep anguish stage* that leads to copious amounts of complaining, bickering, weeping, and gnashing of teeth across the nation; third is the *chicanery stage* in which regional fits of out-and-out bribery and horse-trading to hustle a BTAC or two break out; and fourth is the *forbearance stage*, meaning the sad embracing of the reality that most consumers will never taste the BTAC. Any Kentucky whiskey distiller toiling in the depressed 1970s or 1980s could never conceive of the time or circumstance in which this type of reaction to a five-bottle collection of bourbon and rye could occur. But in 2021, this is where we are.

The BTAC program was unveiled in 2000, with the inaugural collection totaling only three whiskeys that were priced at $49.99 each, Sazerac 18-Year-Old, Eagle Rare 17-Year-Old, and William Larue Weller 19-Year-Old. The reaction from the media was robust and positive from the very first release. Over the subsequent four years, the roster was juggled like tennis balls in the hands of Zippy the circus clown. The 2005 BTAC, for instance, boasted three individual George T. Stagg bottlings, which from a marketing standpoint made little sense and, in fact, seeded confusion in the marketplace, which was still adjusting to the concept of high-priced super-premium American whiskey. The quintet that we still see and covet today in 2021 was settled on in 2006.

Recollected Mark Brown about how the George T. Stagg element of the Antique Collection came to be, "A barrel-strength whiskey was then suggested by a West Virginia consumer. We did not think, to be honest, it would sell but were prepared to give it a shot. The whiskey was conceived and picked by a group of Buffalo Trace retirees, all in their 80s and 90s, including legends like Jimmy Johnson and Orville Schupp."

Master distiller Harlen Wheatley talked to me about the BTAC program's earliest days in our interview, "I remember when we launched the collection . . . it was an evolution in the first years. From the production side, it was the Sazerac 18-Year-Old [rye] that was first. I remember the conversation about Stagg [laughs] and someone from marketing questioning, 'But who's going to be willing to buy an uncut, unfiltered whiskey?' To me, the collection is the halo of all that we do with making whiskey. They are the best offerings of our various recipes . . . each recipe for each edition checks all the boxes for what you want in either a great rye or bourbon . . . the variety is the key element that makes it [BTAC] special."

Echoed Mark Brown in an email to me last October, "The consistent critical acclaim that our Antique Collection whiskeys have won on the global stage over the past 20 years has helped to elevate the status of American whiskey and Buffalo Trace Distillery. Which we believe is both justified and helpful to the development of the entire category. Making a fine bottle of bourbon or rye is every bit as complicated and stressful as making the world's finest French Bordeaux . . ."

But, will the small quantities of the BTAC forever be a fact of life? What about introducing new bourbons or ryes? Replied Brown, "We have been laying away more Antique Collection barrels so we are pleased that we will be able to bring more to consumers in coming years. We do not have any current plans to add new expressions."

In 2021, when the predictable controversies abound as to which American whiskey is the best of the best, it can come as no surprise that a Van Winkle or Antique Collection expression is frequently cited. This sort of exercise is, in my own view as a been-around-the-block spirits critic and writer, a pointless expenditure of gray matter energy. You will receive no argument from me concerning the quality of the Van Winkle, The Last Drop, or Antique Collection whiskeys. As advertised, they are each of unimpeachable pedigree, masterfully crafted and aged, and often are stupendously charming whiskeys. But, to lay claim that this rye or that bourbon is the finest American whiskey of all when in recent years there have existed so many wonderful bourbons, ryes, bottled in bonds, single barrels, small batches, single malts, and more domestic whiskeys produced both by mainstream and craft distillers is absurd, parochial, and myopic. Face it: such an exercise is always floated on the vast and undulating ocean of subjectivity.

So, here's a personal hint from me to thee: the best American whiskey is not necessarily the one that the critics and the bloggers rave about. It's actually the one that happens to be the whiskey that *you* prefer the most.

Freddie Johnson's Promise

Buffalo Trace Distillery's line-up of key managers rings with the widely respected names of seasoned beverage industry veterans led by CEO Mark Brown, master distiller Harlen Wheatley, public relations manager Amy Preske, master blender and director of quality Drew Mayville, and marketing services director Meredith Moody. But, when it comes to which employee comes face-to-face with the most consumers on a yearly basis, that distinction goes to Freddie Johnson.

Freddie Johnson, since 2002 a tour guide at Buffalo Trace Distillery, was born in Paris, Kentucky. Freddie represents the third generation of the Johnson family to be employed by the distilling company now known as Buffalo Trace Distillery. The Johnson family tree has roots that extend back to the end of slavery in the United States. Freddie's ancestor Martha worked as a cook for the owner, a Colonel West, of a plantation located near the distillery site.

James "Jimmy" Johnson, Sr., Freddie's grandfather, was hired in 1912 and worked in the distillery and warehouses when Albert Blanton was distillery manager. Making his own history along the way, Jimmy Sr. became Kentucky's first African-American warehouse foreman. He also traveled occasionally with Blanton on business trips. Blanton's faith in Jimmy Johnson, Sr., was so complete that he entrusted him with the management and welfare of 150,000 barrels of whiskey.

In 1936, then, it was hardly a surprise that Jimmy's son, Jimmy Jr. joined his father at the age of 20. Soon to be noticed was one of Jimmy Jr.'s uncanny abilities. He had the knack of being able to delicately repair warehoused barrels that had sprung leaks without disturbing the barrel's contents. Widely respected within the industry like his father, Jimmy Jr. ascended to the role of warehouse supervisor.

Freddie, Jimmy Jr.'s son, made his initial visit to the distillery with his father and grandfather when he was five and was immediately enthralled with the machinery, the sounds and aromas, and the magical inner workings of the riverside distillery. Freddie's relentless curiosity with all things mechanical led him to try his hand at tinkering with electrical circuitry. While in the eighth grade, he created a model that caught the attention of a teacher, who encouraged him to enter his project into a competition operated by the local 4-H organization. He won. In fact, Freddie won a succession of competitions that propelled him to compete in a national contest held in Washington, D.C. This eventually led to him later on being enrolled in the Management Development Program of AT&T after his stint at Kentucky State University in his hometown of Frankfort. Freddie's career path with AT&T from 1968 to the 1990s wound its way over the years to working on network operations engineering and fiber-optics projects with Bell Labs and Lucent Technologies. Then came a phone call in 2001 from his dad Jimmy Jr.

"When I was small," recalled Freddie in a 2020 interview, "I remember my father saying to me, 'Freddie, if anything ever happens to me, will you be my caretaker?'" Freddie promised his father that he would. Pleased, Jimmy Jr. continued, "When I make this phone call, I'll need you to come home, Son." Responded Freddie, "Of course, Dad."

Freddie's father also expressed his wish that his talented son would someday work at Buffalo Trace, closing the circle started in 1912 by Jimmy Sr. After receiving the call from Jimmy Jr., Freddie decided to take an early retirement from AT&T and soon returned to Frankfort to look after his father.

Since 2002, Freddie has been a popular tour guide at Buffalo Trace Distillery and today is its Distillery VIP Visitor Lead. Many thousands of visitors – 293,996 total in pre-pandemic 2019 – each year get to learn about the old Leestown site, bourbon and how it's made and aged, through the informative and entertaining tours captained by Freddie Johnson. So compelling is Freddie as a tour guide that he has been showered with several awards, including being inducted into the Kentucky Bourbon Hall of Fame in 2018. All this is due to Freddie keeping the solemn promise he had made decades ago about answering a call, which was the honorable thing, the only thing, to do.

17

"... Projecting Forecasts in 2020 for the Next 100, 120 Years ..."

WITH THE CHARACTERS of eras past acting as specter-like guides, CEO Mark Brown and master distiller Harlen Wheatley have set Buffalo Trace Distillery on an ambitious course of unprecedented accomplishments and aspirations in the twenty-first century. The distillery's achievements, not just in winning bushels of medals and awards in spirits competitions conducted around the globe, but of increased market share, of collecting production data through intricate and costly experimental programs, and of brand and distillery acquisitions positions the company in the apex within the Kentucky whiskey industry.

As the new century advanced, Buffalo Trace in one instance found itself to be the beneficiary of random good fortune, such as when the headlines squawked about the discovery of the "Bourbon Pompeii" in publications from *Food & Wine* to the *Northern Kentucky Tribune* to the

Miami Herald. The hubbub began with the accidental discovery in early 2016 of one of E.H. Taylor, Jr.'s O.F.C. distillery edifices that had been built in 1883 after the catastrophic fire of 1882. The twenty-first-century renovations, designed to shore up the riverside structure, were taking place for the purpose of creating a new two-floor event space located on distillery property.

As the workers hammered through a concrete floor in April of 2016, they discovered a series of brick structures. Halting the reconstruction, the opinion arose between the workers and the Buffalo Trace team that what lay below the floor might be of historical significance. After whiskey historian Carolyn Brooks and bourbon archaeologist Nicolas Laracuente were summoned to view the excavation, the determination was made that the workers had come across a significant find directly linked to the O.F.C. Distillery. At that point, the renovations were suspended indefinitely. By June, it was clear that the find turned out to be a series of Taylor's 11,000-gallon copper-lined fermenters. Taylor, who if you recall was the major proponent of the use of copper in whiskey distillation, wrote in 1883, "The fermenting room of the O.F.C. distillery is believed to be the handsomest and best in America . . . The vats, eight in number, are constructed of brick, laid in English cement – the base six feet below the level of the floor, and the tops 11 feet below the ceiling. They are first lined with the first quality of Portland cement, and this again lined with the *best sheet copper,* manufactured especially for the purpose."[1] The use of italics for emphasis came from Taylor himself.

Archaeologist Nicolas Laracuente went on to say he believed that "the tanks are almost certainly the only ones of their kind in existence at any Kentucky distillery."[2] Mark Brown, being no rookie in the skill of attracting media attention, crowed about finding the "eighth wonder of the world." Soon the verbal identifiers "Bourbon Pompeii" adhered to the fermenter story that was widely covered in local and national trade media. Of course, comparing the find of E.H. Taylor, Jr.'s century-and-a-half old fermenters to those of the excavations that unearthed the ash-caked city of Pompeii, Italy, after the massive volcanic eruption of Mount Vesuvius in 79 CE on the surface seemed outlandish. But, the message's subtext of planting the seeds of an intriguing American heartland tale was laden with media savvy.

With the original event space plans scrapped in favor of highlighting the archaeological bonanza, in January of 2019 E.H. Taylor, Jr.'s fermenter was filled with sour mash and connected with new piping to a small still. As of this time of writing, tours were being conducted on a reservation-only basis on a series of catwalks resting over the fermenters. Sometimes luck just finds you when things are going well.

But this recent episode spotlights how savvy Buffalo Trace's management team is in seizing opportunities, sometimes pivoting away from previous plans, and in the process creating a windfall of media exposure. Commented American whiskey blogger Chuck Cowdery about Buffalo Trace/Sazerac's corporate agility in an interview with me in the fall of 2020, "Because, like their competitor Heaven Hill, Sazerac is a privately owned firm whose crown jewel is Buffalo Trace, they have the ability to make decisions quickly and effectively as opposed to other large companies, say like Diageo, Brown Forman or Beam Suntory, who by their very corporate structure have to answer to stockholders, go through the committee process and, therefore, are not as free to make on-the-spot decisions or course corrections as a family-owned company . . . There's no beverage industry executive who's better at dealing with spontaneity than Mark Brown."

Preparing for What's Next . . . with Caution

Even in a disconcerting era, complete with the recent crippling effects of the COVID-19 pandemic such as regional lockdowns, the resultant economic uncertainty, wildly fluctuating international tariffs, and domestic civil discord, Sazerac/Buffalo Trace and the big players in the American whiskey industry are nevertheless preparing for a promising, if fragile future. While the craft distilling industry in the United States, by stark contrast, suffered significant losses in the final nine months of 2020 (a 41 percent falloff in sales by late August of 2020 for a loss of an estimated $700 million, according to *Forbes*), Buffalo Trace Distillery and other sizeable American distillers remained bullish as they continued to bet heavily on sustained marketplace progress by investing in infrastructure.

In the fall of 2020, reports in such respected news sources as *The Spirits Business*, *drinksbusiness*, and *Industry Today* were breaking down the stunning dollar expenditures. These corporate leaps of faith were based mostly on recent buying habits and their likely pathways in the future. For example, the reputable Distilled Spirits Council of the United States (DISCUS) statistics in early 2020 noted that the American whiskey category grew by an eye-popping 10.8 percent in 2019. The data pointed out further that these figures were fueled by the buying public interest over the five-year period of 2014–2019 in premium (+37 percent) and super-premium (+147 percent) spirits brands. These data go a long way in explaining why Buffalo Trace Distillery whiskeys like Old Rip Van Winkle, W.L. Weller, the Buffalo Trace Antique Collection, E.H. Taylor, Jr., Blanton's, and more are as scarce as tap-dancing wolverines dressed in lederhosen. In early 2021 as this book was being completed, Nielsen surveys reported that sales of distilled spirits in 2020 rose by 25.1 percent.

In addition to the $1.2 billion expansion currently going on at the Buffalo Trace campus, rival Diageo is spending $130 million on a new distillery in Lebanon, Kentucky, in which they will produce their popular brand of bourbon and rye, Bulleit. Beam Suntory has broken ground on the new Fred B. Noe Craft Distillery, which is part of a $60 million commitment to rejuvenate its property at their traditional home base in Clermont, Kentucky. Pernod Ricard meanwhile has re-entered the American whiskey arena after selling off Wild Turkey to Gruppo Campari in 2009 by purchasing the craft distillery TX of Fort Worth, Texas, Rabbit Hole Whiskey of Louisville, Kentucky, Smooth Ambler West Virginian Whiskey, and Castle Brands, the producers of Jefferson's Bourbon. Not to be outdone, Heaven Hill Distilleries of Bardstown, Kentucky, was reported in 2020 to be spending $17.5 million to expand and rebrand their popular attraction, the Bourbon Heritage Center, and Brown Forman is slated to drop $96 million on distillery expansion. Even "smaller" distilleries, like Uncle Nearest of Shelbyville, Tennessee, were said to be in the process of developing $50 million worth of investment capital on expansion plans. The St. Louis–based drinks firm Luxco, bought by MGPI, in 2018 built a distillery called Lux Row Distillers in Bardstown, Kentucky, for $35 million.

In the wake of the COVID-19 outbreak in March of 2020, the intentions and projects of some companies, especially those in the craft category, have yet to materialize as this book was going to press. As was reported in *The Spirits Business* on October 27, 2020, "The pandemic looks likely to have a larger impact on the smaller players as major firms forge on with expansion plans. [Luxco executive Greg] Mefford believes the rapid expansion of craft distilleries in the US will plateau in the current climate . . . 'Now would not be the time to build a small-time craft distillery.'"[3]

That said, the dollar amounts that have been invested over the past five years in facility upgrades, the development of new brands, the construction of new distilleries, and brand acquisitions by the major companies that all pertain to American whiskey are unprecedented. The stark reality is that while Buffalo Trace has without a doubt led the expansion race, its competitors have not been sitting on their hands. This state of affairs does not rile Mark Brown, however, who sees this growth in optimistic terms. "The expansion by many of our competitors doesn't affect us at all. It, in fact, makes us realize that the steps we are taking are the correct ones for the time we live in. It all goes to confirm our belief in the future of bourbon."

And as for the future of Buffalo Trace's parent company, Sazerac, whiskey blogger Chuck Cowdery thinks that it will be fine, saying, "We always talk about Diageo, Beam Suntory, Pernod Ricard as being industry leaders but I have to believe that Sazerac ranks right up there . . . Diageo was built by acquisitions and then they'd shed 50 brands here, 10 brands there, often to Heaven Hill and then they'd take what they wanted and then sell what they didn't want to Luxco. Sazerac followed a similar pattern but they made the most with the key brands that they kept . . . I think that Sazerac has improved the existing model by bringing greater profitability than some of their competitors. Mark Brown lives by a 'conventional wisdom, be damned' strategy that has worked well for them. Under his leadership they've [Sazerac] become one of the largest companies in the industry. He's been very successful and he's done it his way."

Yet the "conventional wisdom, be damned" approach can supply the burrs found beneath some people's saddles. As one can imagine when one player in a game of Texas hold 'em is enjoying a crazy run and is winning small towers of blue-colored chips, the opinions of his or her table partners can vary from smoldering envy to incendiary fury. Take Buffalo Trace's controversial stance with the Kentucky Distillers' Association, for example. Established in 1880, the non-profit KDA was, to quote it directly, "founded . . . to unite the Commonwealth's signature Bourbon industry, promote our amber art around the world and protect its enduring spirit from those who would do it harm." Those are lofty ideals to be sure, even if presented with a dash of purple prose.

The KDA isn't the only such trade organization in the global spirits category. Scotland's Scotch Whisky Association does much the same in terms of oversight duties, but with bagpipes, haggis, and the alluring background of Blair Castle. The SWA was founded in 1942 and today no less than 95 percent of Scotland's whisky distillers are members. And cognac, the world famous French grape brandy, has its own association version, the Bureau National Interprofessionnel du Cognac (BNIC). Armagnac, in France's Gascony region, has the Bureau National Interprofessionnel de l'Armagnac (BNIA). Then, of course, there is DISCUS, the Distilled Spirits Council of the United States, which represents large and small beverage firms who distill spirits. Beverage industry trade associations serve many purposes, from creating a sense of unity and camaraderie to lobbying legislative bodies for more favorable laws to public relations to hosting frivolous parties, which, as I know from direct experience, can be remarkably silly. Some association efforts produce serious and beneficial results; other activities are purely cosmetic. That's the game of it.

The rub concerning the KDA/Buffalo Trace disagreement is that while virtually all of Buffalo Trace's primary competitors are members, including Brown Forman, Wild Turkey, Heaven Hill, Four Roses, Diageo, Beam Suntory, Michter's, Bardstown Bourbon Company, Lux Row Distillers, and more, Mark Brown has taken the stance that he and Buffalo Trace are not interested in participating. "We resigned in 2009," public relations manager Amy Preske told me. "Dues are based on the number of barrels one has in their warehouses. We don't think that's fair. We decided that we'd rather put those funds towards the marketing of our own brands rather than paying dues . . . and yes, we are looked upon as renegades.

Public Relations Manager Amy Preske

There is some competitive jealousy, I think." Under further questioning Preske acknowledged that there was "friction between the KDA and Buffalo Trace that centered around the leadership."

Mark Brown explained his position in crisp terms to me through an email exchange in October of 2020 when I asked him why he prefers to go his own way. "It is very simple," he wrote, "a) we do not agree with KDA policy positions on any number of issues, b) we believe the dues structure is wrong, and c) we are not supportive of its executive leadership choice."

In the interest of hearing both sides, I contacted Eric Gregory, the president of the KDA, to obtain his viewpoint after hearing those offered with candor by the Buffalo Trace hierarchy. Gregory did not directly address the Buffalo Trace posture in his diplomatic response. Instead, he wrote me four paragraphs outlining the KDA's history, enumerating a laundry list of statistics pointing to the value of the association, which represents 40 distillers based in Kentucky. Gregory assured me in the final paragraph that ". . . the KDA maintains an open membership policy and just completed its annual drive to educate and invite non-members, including Sazerac, on the many benefits of membership . . ." Nothing to see here. Keep moving.

And, Finally, about Those Awards and What They Really Mean

From the Pleistocene epoch to the present day, a journey covering 12,000 years has brought us to the moment when the matter of how Buffalo Trace Distillery has become the world's most awarded whiskey distillery in modern history requires an objective accounting. When viewing the official company website's summary of the awards, honors, and accolades bestowed upon 26 of the whiskeys, one whiskey liqueur, and a vodka produced at the distillery, one begins to comprehend the scope of what has been achieved since 1997, the year that Mark Brown returned to the Sazerac Company fold. The distillery's namesake whiskey Buffalo Trace Kentucky Straight Bourbon, called "a tremendous value" by blogger Chuck Cowdery and a "very versatile bourbon" by critics Michael Veach and Susan Reigler, has alone been the recipient of over one hundred honors from a host of the world's foremost spirits contests, publications, and journalists since its introduction in 2000. As of late 2020, the total number of awards for Buffalo Trace's whiskey portfolio exceeds one thousand. In a tally gleaned from the data offered by the other large beverage alcohol mega-companies, I believe Buffalo Trace's claim that they have indeed won more awards than any other distillery in the world.

The long trail of media recognition started with a bang in 2000 when *The Malt Advocate* (today *Whisky Advocate*, published by M. Shaken Communications) named Buffalo Trace as the Distillery of the Year. A parade of media-generated accolades followed, including 2010 Visitor Attraction of the Year (*Whisky Magazine*), 2011 Brand Innovator of the Year (*Whisky Magazine*), 2014 Distillery of the Year, America (*Whisky Magazine*), 2017

Visitor Attraction of the Year (*Whisky Magazine*), in 2018 the same year that Buffalo Trace celebrated producing its seven millionth barrel of bourbon since Prohibition, Distillery of the Year/Icons of Whisky (*Whisky Magazine*), and in 2020 the Distillery of the Year award at the San Francisco World Spirits Competition.

Skeptics could argue without the benefit of close examination that by producing 450 brands and submitting many of them to the 40 to 50 spirits contests held around the world each year that the sheer mathematics would work in Sazerac/Buffalo Trace's favor. Not true, counters Amy Preske, saying, "First of all, we only enter competitions that are reputable and completely above board. We are very careful about where our submissions go. Plus, even acknowledging our large portfolio, the majority of Sazerac Company's products are never entered at all, as we prefer instead to have our premium and super-premium spirits evaluated, in particular our whiskey portfolio, by objective sources."

Therefore, to understand fully what the Buffalo Trace Distillery has accomplished on its own it is vital to keep separate what Sazerac's crown jewel property does from the dealings of its parent company. The awards roster in question does not include the honors won by other Sazerac whiskey distilleries, such as A. Smith Bowman, 1792 Barton, Old Montreal Distillery, Glenmore Distillery, Popcorn Sutton Distillery, and others. It is the resultant two-decade outcome from the distillery in Frankfort, Kentucky, alone that is the core message here. But make no mistake. The collecting of an impressive number of awards and medals from a total of less than one hundred submitted products carries with it sobering effects, including the pressure to keep on winning.

Said Harlen Wheatley of winning so many hundreds of awards and medals for the whiskeys he and his team produce, "The awards clarify things . . . they act as affirmations, or not, from independent sources and educated palates that perhaps we're really on the right track, still going in the right direction."

Amy Preske had a different perspective from her coworkers, addressing what the medals and awards mean for the employees of Buffalo Trace. "What do the awards mean? They are a key driver for company morale. Winning a gold medal or a chairman's trophy or a best of show accolade resonates with the people who work each day on the bottling line or the groundskeepers who mow the lawns. It signals to them that we're a united team that's always striving to be better, striving for excellence from the top down. And besides, there's Mark [Brown], who is highly competitive and endlessly curious."

Amy Preske's use of the descriptor *curious* rang a bell in my memory when I heard it. When in the early 2000s I was writing *A Double Scotch* I asked Edgar Bronfman, Sr., in an interview about what personality trait he believed had most made his father, Samuel Bronfman, who led the iconic company Joseph E. Seagram & Sons, the twentieth-century's undisputed "Camelot of beverage alcohol," he replied simply, "Curiosity. My father always made the point that more than any other character trait curiosity was mandatory for success." Consequently, the outcome of Bronfman's curiosity was a company culture that exuded professionalism, forward thinking, and unadulterated success.

After two years of research, conducting tens of interviews, and writing, my conclusion is that Buffalo Trace Distillery is the world's most awarded distillery for two reasons: first, the long line of innovators and distillers since 1870 that left indelible impressions and, second, Mark Brown's deft and nimble leadership. His ability to hire motivated and experienced women and men and then sagely allow them the freedom and the resources to be creative and enterprising is the critical component. Further, Brown's competitive nature and unrelenting quest for brilliance and pertinent data at all levels of operation is rewriting how whiskey producers need to approach the challenges of twenty-first-century distillery operation. There is a palpable Buffalo Trace culture that has evolved over the two decades of his tenure. That corporate culture echoes the twentieth-century glory years of 1950 to the late 1990s when Joseph E. Seagram reigned supreme in North America and on the international stage.

As history has depicted, the American whiskey industry is prone to fierce cyclical gyrations. Yet, it remains to some extent a massive domestic trade that to its detriment treasures bland continuity, obsolete ritual, and, worst of all, playing it safe. As Harlen Wheatley told me last year about his team's data gathering through experimentation, "Because our industry is so cyclical, we're projecting forecasts in 2020 for the next 100,

The Buffalo Trace Distillery campus today

120 years so that we can minimize the effects of the cycles that undoubt-edly lie ahead." The dreaded obstacles endured in the first half of the twentieth century and then subsequently during the 30-year "dark ages" period of 1970–2000 bore witness to an industry being unprepared to cope and adapt.

Mark Brown and his Buffalo Trace management team give every indi-cation that they are motivated neither by ego, nor by conventional wis-dom, nor by the shape-shifting opinions of their competitors or of trade associations, but by a fathomless well of curiosity that nurtures creative, insightful, and progressive planning. Mistakes may be made along the way, they fully acknowledge. But occasional missteps are viewed not as errors so much as they are part of the learning experience. They do not appear to accept as options either running in place or the wasting of time by peering backwards. Resting on laurels is frowned upon. Theirs is an infectious thirst for knowledge that when viewed from the outside can be interpreted as being either an illuminating way forward or as being just a little bit short of crazy. And maybe their quixotic goal of discovering the bourbon Holy Grail will never happen. In a way, I hope they don't discover it so they continue to reach new heights. Or, perhaps the ideal bourbon has been found already in the minds and hearts of some whiskey lovers.

No matter, because this one thing I have come to know: The seed of Buffalo Trace Distillery's riveting quest for perfection first sprang to life when E.H. Taylor, Jr. returned from his European tour, flush with visions of copper shining in each corner of his new, state-of-the-art whiskey distillery, O.F.C. This unquenchable passion for excellence continued in earnest under the regimes of George T. Stagg, Albert Blanton, Orville Schupp, Gary Gayheart, and Elmer T. Lee. All indications point to this adventure continuing, as it unfolds on the National Landmark site where for millennia migrating buffalo carved a riverbank trough, a crossing on the Kentucky River that the Shawnee called *Atlanant-o-wamiowee*, "the buffalo trace."

Appendix

PRESENTED FOR YOUR imbibing pleasure is a brief summary of the quality levels of Buffalo Trace Distillery's award-winning range of distillates, the vast majority of which are whiskey, produced in Frankfort, Kentucky. Rather than offering detailed tasting notes on each selection, I instead have chosen to feature an overall ranking of each, grouped as *Recommended, Highly Recommended,* and *Highest Recommendation.* These critical assessments, strictly my own, are drawn from scores of recent evaluations, none more than three years old.

Buffalo Trace Distillery Whiskeys and Spirits

Highest Recommendation: Benchmark Quality

- Antique Collection George T. Stagg Kentucky Straight Bourbon
- Antique Collection Thomas H. Handy Sazerac Straight Rye
- Antique Collection William Larue Weller Kentucky Straight Bourbon
- Blanton's Single Barrel Kentucky Straight Bourbon
- Col. E.H. Taylor, Jr. Barrel Proof Kentucky Straight Bourbon
- Col. E.H. Taylor, Jr. Bottled-in-Bond Warehouse C Tornado Surviving Kentucky Straight Bourbon
- Col. E.H. Taylor, Jr. Single Barrel Bottled-in-Bond Kentucky Straight Bourbon

- O.F.C. Vintage Kentucky Straight Bourbon
- Pappy Van Winkle 15-Year-Old Kentucky Straight Bourbon
- Pappy Van Winkle 20-Year-Old Kentucky Straight Bourbon
- Stagg, Jr. Kentucky Straight Bourbon

Highly Recommended: Very Good Quality

- Antique Collection Eagle Rare 17-Year-Old Kentucky Straight Bourbon
- Antique Collection Sazerac Rye 18-Year-Old Kentucky Straight Rye
- Buffalo Trace Kentucky Straight Bourbon
- Col. E.H. Taylor, Jr. Bottled-in-Bond Four Grain Kentucky Straight Bourbon
- Col. E.H. Taylor, Jr. Bottled-in-Bond Amaranth Kentucky Straight Bourbon
- Col. E.H. Taylor, Jr. Bottled-in-Bond Kentucky Straight Rye
- Col. E.H. Taylor, Jr. Small Batch Bottled-in-Bond Kentucky Straight Bourbon
- Col. E.H. Taylor, Jr. Bottled-in-Bond Cured Oak Kentucky Straight Bourbon
- Col. E.H. Taylor, Jr. Bottled-in-Bond Seasoned Oak Kentucky Straight Bourbon
- Col. E.H. Taylor, Jr. Bottled-in-Bond Old Fashioned Sour Mash
- Eagle Rare Kentucky Straight Bourbon
- Elmer T. Lee Single Barrel Kentucky Straight Bourbon
- Old Rip Van Winkle 10-Year-Old Handmade Kentucky Straight Bourbon
- Old Rip Van Winkle Special Reserve 12-Year-Old Kentucky Straight Bourbon
- Old Rip Van Winkle Family Reserve 13-Year-Old Kentucky Straight Rye

- Pappy Van Winkle 23-Year-Old Kentucky Straight Bourbon
- Wheatley Vodka
- W.L. Weller C.Y.P.B. Kentucky Straight Bourbon
- W.L. Weller Full Proof Kentucky Straight Bourbon
- W.L. Weller 12-Year-Old Kentucky Straight Bourbon

Recommended: Good Quality

- Ancient Ancient Age 10 Star Kentucky Straight Bourbon
- Benchmark Old No. 8 Brand Kentucky Straight Bourbon
- Buffalo Trace Distillery Bourbon Cream Liqueur
- Buffalo Trace White Dog Wheated Mash
- Buffalo Trace White Dog Rye Mash
- Old Charter French Oak Kentucky Straight Bourbon
- Old Charter 8 Kentucky Straight Bourbon
- Old Charter Canadian Oak Kentucky Straight Bourbon
- Old Charter Mongolian Oak Kentucky Straight Bourbon
- Sazerac Rye Kentucky Straight Rye
- W.L. Weller Special Reserve Kentucky Straight Bourbon
- W.L. Weller Antique 107 Kentucky Straight Bourbon

Author's note: Please be aware that as of the writing of this book, many of these lovely spirits, primarily the whiskeys, are so fervently sought after that their distribution may be on an allocation basis. This means that because they are of a finite nature, release to release, their supply may not be sufficient to the enthusiastic demand and, therefore, their quantities are likely to be meted out, region to region. We all wish this wasn't the case, but the current reality dictates that no other measure than this can be taken.

Timeline

10,000 BCE (circa): Laurentide Glacier recedes into Canada; Pleistocene Epoch.

9500–8000 BCE: Bison species survives North American Pleistocene megafauna extinction.

8000–1000 BCE: Central North America turns more habitable for indigenous peoples.

1000 BCE–1000 CE: Tribal communities become established in Kentucky/Ohio region.

1609: Western reaches of Virginia colony claimed by King James I of England.

1650–1675: Initial Euro-American explorations of region that includes Kentucky occur.

1750–1800: Western movement into Kentucky to build settlements begins in earnest.

1773: McAfee brothers and Hancock Taylor survey the area around and including "the great buffalo trace."

1775: Willis Lee and Captain Hancock Lee survey and roughly map out Leestown.

1786: After receiving full title, Hancock Lee establishes Leestown. General James Wilkinson establishes the city of Frankfort.

1792: Kentucky becomes the 15th state.

1818: Kentucky legislature allots $10,000 to study navigational abilities of Kentucky River. Inventory at Leestown warehouse includes 1,347 barrels of whiskey.

1830: Edmund Haynes Taylor is born.

1835: George T. Stagg is born.

1840: Merchant's Exchange Coffee House opens in New Orleans, later in 1852 to be renamed Sazerac Coffee-House.

1856: Daniel Swigert buys acreage at Leestown.

1857: Swigert builds a modest distillery, the initial whiskey-making facility at the site.

1861–1865: U.S. Civil War.

1870: Col. E.H. Taylor, Jr. purchases the Leestown site and its small distillery; Thomas H. Handy buys Sazerac Coffee-House.

1872: Construction begins on O.F.C. (Old Fired Copper) Distillery at Leestown site.

1874: Julian Prentice "Pappy" Van Winkle is born.

1878: George T. Stagg buys O.F.C. Distillery from the Taylor family; Thomas H. Handy sells Sazerac Coffee-House.

1879: George T. Stagg renames the firm, E.H. Taylor, Jr. Company.

1882: Lightning strike causes catastrophic fire at O.F.C.

1883: O.F.C. rebuilt; construction supervised by E.H. Taylor, Jr.

1885: E.H. Taylor, Jr. resigns from O.F.C.

1886: E.H. Taylor, Jr. joins his sons at J. Swigert Taylor Distillery and forms E.H. Taylor & Sons.

1893: George T. Stagg dies at 57 years of age; Thomas H. Handy dies.

1897: Bottled-in-Bond Act passed by the United States Congress.

1919: Elmer T. Lee is born.

1920: Prohibition dawns; George T. Stagg Distillery remains open to store whiskey and to produce medicinal whiskey.

1923: Edmund Haynes Taylor, Jr. dies at the age of 92.

1929: Schenley Products Company, guided by Lewis Rosenstiel, buys George T. Stagg Distillery.

1933: Prohibition ends.

1937: January rains result in cataclysmic flood in entire Ohio River Valley.

1948: Stephen Goldring of Magnolia Liquor Company acquires New Orleans-based Sazerac Company.

1952: Albert Bacon Blanton retires. Orville Schupp becomes plant manager.

1953: George T. Stagg celebrates 2 million barrels of whiskey produced after Prohibition.

1957: Orville Schupp leaves George T. Stagg.

1959: Albert Bacon Blanton dies at the age of 78.

1964: Old Stagg Kentucky Straight Bourbon passes 200 million bottles sold.

1965: Julian Prentice "Pappy" Van Winkle dies at the age of 91.

1969: Elmer T. Lee named George T. Stagg plant manager.

1976: Lewis Rosenstiel dies at age 84.

1982: Schenley sells George T. Stagg Distillery and its brand Ancient Age to Ferdie Falk and Robert Baranaskas; company is renamed Age International; William Goldring becomes president of Sazerac Company.

1984: Blanton's Single Barrel Kentucky Straight Bourbon Whiskey is launched primarily for Japanese market.

1985: Elmer T. Lee retires as Master Distiller Emeritus from Age International.

1992: Sazerac Company buys George T. Stagg Distillery, managed by Gary Gayheart, and its whiskey inventory.

1994: Gary Gayheart hires Harlen Wheatley.

1997: William Goldring hires Mark Brown, who becomes president and CEO.

1999: George T. Stagg Distillery renamed Buffalo Trace Distillery; Gary Gayheart named master distiller; Buffalo Trace Kentucky Straight Bourbon brand introduced.

2000: Buffalo Trace Antique Collection introduced.

2002: Sazerac Company enters into joint venture with Van Winkle family.

2013: Elmer T. Lees dies at age 93.

2016: Sazerac Company purchases The Last Drop Company.

2018: Buffalo Trace Distillery celebrates seven million barrels of whiskey produced after Prohibition.

1989–2021: Through decades of acquisitions and joint venture associations, Sazerac Company has 450 brands, seven distillery complexes in its massive portfolio, and employs 2,600 people.

Notes

Chapter 1 "This river runes north west and out of ye westerly side . . ."

1. John R. Kennedy. "Salt Licks." In *Encyclopedia of North Carolina*. The University of North Carolina Press, 2006.
2. Clarence W. Alvord and Lee Bidgood. *The First Explorations of the Trans-Allegheny Region by the Virginians, 1650–1674*, Cleveland, OH: The Arthur H. Clark Company, 1912, pp. 209–226.
3. R. P. Stephen Davis, Jr. (ed.). "The Travels of James Needham and Gabriel Arthur through Virginia, North Carolina and Beyond, 1673–1674," *Southern Indian Studies* 39 (October 1990): 31–55.
4. Alan Vance Briceland. *Westward from Virginia: The Exploration of the Virginia-Carolina Frontier 1650–1710*. University of Virginia Press, 1987.
5. *The Courier Journal of Louisville*. "Kentucky Pioneers: The McAfees Among The Distinguished Men Who First Settle the State: How They Came to the Dark and Bloody Ground and Their Later Adventures." September 9, 1888.
6. Williard R. Jillson. *Pioneer Kentucky*. State Journal Company, 1934, p. 12.
7. John Filson. *The Discovery, Settlement and Present State of Kentucke*. Wilmington, DE: Printed by James Adams, 1784.
8. William Clark. *Journals of the Lewis and Clark Expedition – Volume 8*. Notes from August 29, 1806; the Dakotas. Lincoln: University of Nebraska-Lincoln, 1993.
9. George Imlay. *A Topographical Description of the Western Territory of North America*, Volume II. London, England: J. Debrett, Piccadilly, 1793.
10. John A. Jakle. *Salt on the Ohio Valley Frontier, 1770–1820*. University of Illinois, Urbana, p. 691.
11. Ibid.

12. Edward Albright. *Early History of Middle Tennessee*. Nashville, TN: Brandon Printing Company, 1908, p. 18.
13. John A. Jakle, *The American Bison and The Human Occupance of the Ohio Valley*. Urbana: University of Illinois, pp. 299–305.

Chapter 2 "This Map of Kentucke: drawn from actual observations . . ."

1. Boston Rare Maps. www.bostonraremaps.com.
2. Library of Congress. *American Revolution and Its Era: Maps and Charts of North America and the West Indies:1750–1789*.
3. Steve Preston. "Our Rich History: John Filson: First Kentucky Historian, Forgotten Cincinnati Founder." *Northern Kentucky Tribune*, June 18, 2018.
4. Kentucky Kindred Genealogical Research. *The McAfee Brothers – Early Kentucky Pioneers*. May 19, 2019.
5. Ibid.
6. Mary Willis Woodson and Lucy C. Lee. *History of the Lee Family*. Register of Kentucky State Historical Society, Vol. 1, No. 3, September 1903.
7. *Dr. Jedidiah Morse's The American Geography Map*, London 1794, Kentucky Atlas & Gazetter.
8. Image 91 of *The Journal of Nicholas Cresswell, 1774–1777*, Library of Congress.
9. udge Samuel M. Wilson. Address titled "Leestown – Its Founders and Its History," July 16, 1931, p. 392.
10. Ibid.
11. Lowell H. Harrison and Kames C. Klotter. *A New History of Kentucky*. The University of Kentucky Press, 1997, p. 33.
12. Wilson, "Leestown," p. 392.

Chapter 3 ". . . as crooked as a dog's hind leg . . ."

1. Theodore Roosevelt. *The Winning of the West: From the Alleghenies to the Mississippi – Vols. 1 & 2*. New York: G. P. Putnam & Sons, 1894.
2. Andro Linklater. *An Artist in Treason: The Extraordinary Double Life of General James Wilkinson*. New York: Walker & Company, 2009, p. 3.

3. Alfred Henry Lewis. *An American Patrician, or The Story of Aaron Burr*. Lector House, 2020.
4. Linklater. *An Artist in Treason*, p. 72.
5. *FRANK* magazine, May 24, 2018, Arts & Culture section.
6. Judge Samuel M. Wilson. Address titled "Leestown – Its Founders and Its History," July 16, 1931, p. 392.

Chapter 4 ". . . 10,530 bls. flour; 1374 whiskey; 1984 beef and pork . . ."

1. Journal of the Kentucky House of Representatives, 1818.
2. *The Kentucky Gazette*, October 30, 1818, Kentuckiana Digital Library.
3. Leland Winfield Meyer, PhD. *The Life and Times of Colonel Richard M. Johnson of Kentucky*. New York: Columbia University Press, 1932, pp. 193–196.
4. *The Kentucky Reporter*, May 3, 1820.
5. Franklin County, Kentucky Deed Book 6, p. 89.

Chapter 5 ". . . The machinery is of the best . . . for making copper distilled Whisky."

1. *Western Citizen*. Paris, Kentucky, October 8, 1858.
2. Red Smith. "Spendthrift Farm Mob." *New York Times*, May 6, 1978.
3. Lincoln's Writings: NEH EDSITEment. House Divided Project, hdivided@dickinson.edu. Dickinson College, Carlisle, PA.
4. E. Merton Coulter. *Civil War and Re-adjustment in Kentucky*. Gloucester, MA: Peter Smith Publisher, 1926, pp. 16–17.
5. American Battlefield Trust, "Bitters, Blockades, and the Bluegrass State: Bourbon and the Civil War." www.battlefields.org.
6. Steven Bernstein, essentialcivilwarcurriculum.com/Kentucky-in-the-civil-war-1861-1862.html.
7. Michael Veach. "Bourbon History: Bourbon and the American Civil War." www.bourbonveachdot.com.

Chapter 6 "... Bourbon production ... was at best crude and unreliable ..."

1. The New England Historical and Genealogical Register, Vol. 78–79.
2. Michael R. Veach. "19th Century Distilling Papers at The Filson." The Filson Historical Society News Magazine 6, no. 3 (Fall 2006).
3. Richard Taylor. The Great Crossing: A Historic Journey to Buffalo Trace Distillery. Buffalo Trace Distillery, 2002.
4. Carl Kramer, illustrations by William B. Scott. Capital on the Kentucky: A Two Hundred Year History of Frankfort & Franklin County. Historic Frankfort, 1986.
5. Karl Raitz. Making Bourbon: A Geographical History of Distilling in Nineteenth-Century Kentucky. Lexington, KY: The University Press of Kentucky, 2020, p. 39.
6. Raitz. Making Bourbon, p. 39.
7. Gerald Carson. The Social History of Bourbon: An Unhurried Account of Our Star-Spangled American Drink. Lexington, KY: The University Press of Kentucky, 1963, p. 87.
8. The Tri-Weekly Yeoman, November 17, 1870. The Filson Historical Society, Louisville, KY.

Chapter 7 "... That in consideration of Five Hundred dollars ..."

1. Nancy Lovas, Business Reference and Research Specialist. The Panic of 1873. Library of Congress, August 2017.
2. U.S. Mint History: The Crime of 1873. United States Mint, Office of Corporate Communications, March 22, 2017.
3. Elena Holodny. "144 years ago the stock market shut down for the first time because of a panic – here's what happened." Business Insider, September 20, 2017.
4. "Becoming The Colonel: E.H. Taylor and the Making of a Bourbon Aristocrat, Part II." www.Bowtied-and-Bourboned.com, January 2, 2016.
5. Brian Haara. "Col. E.H. Taylor, Jr. – Running from Creditors in the Summer of '77." www.sippncorn.blogspot.com, August 6, 2014.

6. E.H. Taylor Hay, Jr. Buffalo Trace Oral History Project. Louie B. Nunn Center for Oral History, University of Kentucky Libraries, October 20, 2009.
7. Louisville Courier-Journal, November 1877.
8. Ibid.
9. Louisville Courier-Journal, January 1878.
10. Richard Taylor. *The Great Crossing: A Historic Journey to Buffalo Trace Distillery*. Frankfort, KY: Buffalo Trace Distillery, 2002.
11. "Becoming The Colonel."
12. Louisville Courier-Journal, September 21, 1881.

Chapter 8 "Rev. Dr. McLeod Thanks God for Duffy's Pure Malt Whiskey"

1. Wayne Curtis. "Why Every Drinker Should Know What Bottled-in-Bond Means." The Daily Beast, April 26, 2018.
2. "False Advertising and the Legacy of Duffy's Pure Malt Whiskey." www.sippncorn.blogspot.com, January 8, 2014.
3. Curtis. "Why Every Drinker Should Know What Bottled-in-Bond Means."
4. United States Congressional Record. 54th Congress, Session II, March 3, 1897, Chapter 379.
5. Stacy Kula, Esq. "What the Bottled-in-Bond Act of 1897 Means Today." *Distiller Magazine*, October 1, 2017.

Chapter 9 "The most valuable assistance that we got in St. Louis . . ."

1. John C. Tramazzo. *Bourbon & Bullets: True Stories of Whiskey, War, and Military Service*. The University of Nebraska Press, Potomac Books, 2018, pp. 113, 115–117.
2. Ibid.
3. Ibid.
4. Ibid.
5. "The Trials and Ascent of George T. Stagg." Those Pre-Pro Whiskey Men! Blog. http://pre-prowhiskeymen.blogspot.com/2016/04/the-trials-and-ascent-of-george-t-stagg.html. April 30, 2016,.

6. Ibid.
7. Brian Haara. "The Origin of Col. E.H. Taylor, Jr.'s Signature (As Told By Three Trademark Rulings)." www.sippncorn.blogspot.com. October 9, 2013.
8. Ibid.
9. Ibid.
10. "The Trials and Ascent of George T. Stagg."

Chapter 10 ". . . an early nineteenth century residence situated in the middle of an expansive lawn . . ."

1. John E. Kleber, Editor in Chief. *The Kentucky Encyclopedia*. Lexington: The University Press of Kentucky, 1992, p. 353.
2. Ibid.
3. Becky Riddle. "Kentucky History, O.F.C.-Stagg Distillery." www.explorekyhistory.ky.gov.
4. Albert B. Blanton. The Geo. T. Stagg Company, Leestown. The Filson Historical Society, Louisville, KY, p. 4.
5. National Registry of Historic Places Inventory, nomination form, October 24, 1978, p. 2.
6. Frederick A. Wallis and Hambleton Tapp, A.B., M.A. A Sesqui-Centennial History of Kentucky: A Narrative Historical Edition, Commemorating One Hundred and Fifty Years of Statehood, Preserving the record of the Growth and Development of the Commonwealth, and Chronicling the Genealogical and Memorial Record of its Prominent Families and Personages. The Historical Record Association, 1945.
7. Tim Talbott. "Sites, Slaves, and Soldiers: The Beeches." My Musings on American, African American, Southern, Civil War, Reconstruction, and Public History topics and books Blog. randomthoughtsonhistory.blogspot. com/2013/12/sites-slaves-and-soldiers-beeches.html. Posted December 13, 2013.
8. Richard Taylor. The Great Crossing: A Historic Journey to Buffalo Trace Distillery. Buffalo Trace Distillery, 2002, p. 93.
9. "55 years, 'A Company Man': Colonel Albert Bacon Blanton." Whiskey University, www.whiskeyuniv.com.
10. Daniel Okrent. *Last Call: The Rise and Fall of Prohibition*. New York: Scribner's, 2010, p. 8.
11. Blanton. The Geo. T. Stagg Company, p. 10.

12. Amanda Macias. "Prohibition Began 100 Years Ago – Here's a Look at Its Economic Impact." CNBC, January 17, 2020.
13. Fred Minnick. *Bourbon: The Rise, Fall and Rebirth of an American Whiskey.* Minneapolis, MN: Voyageur Press, 2016, pp. 86–88.
14. Ibid.
15. Blanton. The Geo. T. Stagg Company, Leestown, pp. 4, 10–12.
16. Ibid.
17. Ibid.
18. Ibid.
19. Ibid.
20. "55 years, 'A Company Man.'"
21. Ibid.

Chapter 11 ". . . raised the daily production from 400 to 600 barrels . . ."

1. Amy Mittelman. "Schenley Distillers Corporation." Beer, Women, History, Nursing Blog. AmyMittleman.com. January 18, 2019.
2. National Register of Historic Places – James E. Pepper Distillery. U.S. Department of the Interior, Nomination request. December 31, 2008.
3. The New York Times, January 22, 1967.
4. Schenley History Time Line, www.bourbonenthusiast.com.
5. Ibid.
6. Schenley Distillers Corporation. Baker Library – Bloomberg Center, Harvard Business School.
7. Lexington Herald-Leader, April 13, 1937.
8. Schenley History Time Line.
9. The Schenley News, November 1952.

Chapter 12 "Despite many salacious rumors, he is mostly remembered as . . ."

1. The Schenley News, October 1951.
2. Ibid.
3. Advertisement, Charleston West Virginia Gazette, March 13, 1964.

4. Michael R. Veach. *Kentucky Bourbon Whiskey: An American Heritage.* Lexington: The University Press of Kentucky, 2013, p. 105.

5. Hunter Oatman-Stanford. "Drunk History: The Rise, Fall, and Revival of All-American Whiskey." *Collector's Weekly,* August 12, 2015.

6. Ibid.

7. The Schenley News, July 1953.

8. Amy Mittelman. "Schenley Distillers Corporation." Beer, Women, History, Nursing Blog. AmyMittleman.com. January 18, 2019.

9. Whitney Webb. "Hidden in Plain Sight: The Shocking Origins of the Jeffrey Epstein Case." www.mintpressnews.com, July 18, 2019.

10. Ibid.

11. Ibid.

12. Ibid.

13. Nicholas Gage. The New York Times, February 19, 1971.

14. Webb. "Hidden in Plain Sight."

15. "Bid Lost by Cohn on Estate Role." *The New York Times,* June 25, 1976.

16. Marie Brenner. "How Donald Trump and Roy Cohn's Ruthless Symbiosis Changed America." *Vanity Fair,* August 2017.

17. Chuck Cowdery. "Roy Cohn Was Disbarred for Writing Himself into Lew Rosenstiel's Will." The Chuck Cowdrey Blog, May 2, 2019.

18. Leonard Sloane. *The New York Times,* January 22, 1976.

Chapter 13 "Show up next Monday morning . . ."

1. John C. Tramazzo. *Bourbon & Bullets: True Stories of Whiskey, War, and Military Service.* The University of Nebraska Press, Potomac Books, 2018, pp. 135–138.

2. Chuck Cowdrey. "Is Bourbon Officially America's Native Spirit?" The Chuck Cowdrey Blog, April 27, 2009.

3. Reid Mitenbuler. "How Bourbon Became 'America's Native Spirit.'" Slate – A Dork's Dork, May 2015.

4. Noah Rothbaum. *The Art of American Whiskey: A Visual History of the Nation's Most Storied Spirit, through 100 Iconic Labels.* Berkeley, CA: Ten Speed Press, pp. 104–105.

5. Ibid.

6. Tim McKirdy. "The Surprisingly Short History of Single-Malt Scotch." Vinepair, April 30, 2019.

7. Tom Acitelli. *Whiskey Business: How Small Batch Distillers Are Transforming American Spirits*. Chicago: Chicago Review Press, 2017, p. 120.
8. Schenley History Time Line. www.bourbonenthusiast.com.
9. Fred Minnick. *Bourbon: The Rise, Fall and Rebirth of an American Whiskey*. Minneapolis, MN: Voyageur Press, 2016, p. 193.
10. Acitelli. Whiskey Business, pp. 81–82.
11. Ibid.
12. Elmer T. Lee Journals. SCA 1990 001.tif; Buffalo Trace Distillery archives.
13. Tom Acitelli. *Whiskey Business: How Small Batch Distillers Are Transforming American Spirits*. Chicago: Chicago Review Press, 2017, p. 85.
14. Elmer T. Lee Journals, "Promotional Events." July 1990, SCA 1990 002.tif; Buffalo Trace Distillery archives.
15. Ibid.
16. Ibid.

Chapter 14 Sazerac: The New Company and the Fabled Cocktail

1. Wayne Curtis. "History Lesson: The Sazerac." *Imbibe Magazine*, July 16, 2019.
2. Ian McNulty. "The Crescent City Coffee Connection: History and Heritage Imbues Each Cup." NewOrleansFrenchQuarter.com.
3. "Sazerac Cocktail – A History Revealed." Drinking Cup Blog.
4. Stanley Clisby Arthur. Famous New Orleans Drinks and How to Mix 'Em. Harmanson, 1938.
5. Curtis. History Lesson.
6. Ibid.
7. David Wondrich. *Imbibe! From Absinthe Cocktail to Whiskey Smash, a Salute in Stories and Drinks to "Professor" Jerry Thomas, Pioneer of the American Bar*. New York: Penguin Random House, 2015, pp. 238–239.
8. "A Rich Heritage and an Even Brighter Future." Our Story/Sazerac Company, www.sazerac.com, plate 18.
9. Chuck Cowdery. "The Humble Beginnings of Sazerac's Bourbon Juggernaut." The Chuck Cowdery Blog, chuckcowdery.blogspot.com, April 8, 2016.
10. Becky Paskin. "Brown: Sazerac Remains on Acquisition Trail." *The Spirits Business*, July 16, 2014.
11. Alex Day, Nick Fauchald, and David Kaplan. *Cocktail Codex: Fundamentals, Formulas, Evolutions*. New York: Ten Speed Press, 2018, p. 33.

Chapter 15 "Experimentation is in our DNA . . ."

1. Press release, Buffalo Trace Distillery, April 23, 2020.
2. Knittel, Tim. "The Quest for the Perfect Bourbon." distiller.blog, April 15, 2017.

Chapter 16 "Resistance is futile"

1. Conway, Jan. "Fireball Liqueur's Sales Volume in the U.S. 2013–2019." Statista, September 22, 2020.
2. Sherry, Kristiane, "The Sazerac Company Has Acquired The Last Drop Distillers Limited, a British Family-Run Spirits Bottler, for an Undisclosed Sum." *The Spirits Business*, September 6, 2016.
3. Bruce-Gardyne, Tom. "The Last Drop Distillers: A Brand History." *The Spirits Business*, October 18, 2018.
4. Ibid.
5. Ibid.
6. "Seekers of Rare Spirits: The Last Drop Distillers," Travel, Food & Drink, christiesrealestate.com, December 20, 2019.
7. Paskin, Becky. "Last Drop Distillers Sold To Sazerac." scotchwhisky.com/ magazine, September 6, 2016.
8. "Van Winkle Family Asks Retailers and Resellers to Play Nice," The Chuck Cowdery Blog, October 10, 2019.

Chapter 17 ". . . projecting forecasts in 2020 for the next 100, 120 years . . ."

1. Janet Patton. "Bourbon Pompeii found at Buffalo Trace Distillery." *Lexington Herald Leader*, October 14, 2016.
2. Ibid.
3. *The Spirits Business*. October 27, 2020.

Bibliography

Acetelli, Tom. *Whiskey Business: How Small-Batch Distillers Are Transforming American Spirits*. Chicago: Chicago Review Press, 2017.

Broom, Dave: *Whisky: The Manual*. London: Mitchell Beazley, 2014.

Carson, Gerald. *The Social History of Bourbon: An Unhurried Account of Our Star-Spangled American Drink*. Lexington: The University Press of Kentucky, 1963.

Cecil, Sam K. *Bourbon: The Evolution of Kentucky Whiskey*. New York: Turner Publishing Company, 2010.

Clark, Thomas D. *A History of Kentucky*. Ashland, KY: The Jesse Stuart Foundation, 1988.

Cowdery, Charles. *Bourbon, Straight: The Uncut and Unfiltered Story of American Whiskey*. Chicago: Made and Bottled in Kentucky, 2004.

Cowdery, Charles. *Bourbon, Strange: Surprising Stories of American Whiskey*. Chicago: Made and Bottled in Kentucky, 2014.

Crowgey, Henry G. *Kentucky Bourbon: The Early Years of Whiskeymaking*. Lexington: The University Press of Kentucky, 2008.

Day, Alex, Nick Fauchald, and David Kaplan, with Devon Tarby. *Cocktail Codex: Fundamentals • Formulas • Evolutions*. New York: Ten Speed Press, 2018.

DeGroff, Dale. *The New Craft of the Cocktail: Everything You Need to Know to Think Like a Master Mixologist, with 500 Recipes*. New York: Clarkson Potter, 2020.

Givens, Ron. *Bourbon at Its Best: The Lore & Allure of America's Finest Spirits*. Cincinnati, OH: Clerisy Press, 2008.

Harrison, Lowell H., and James C. Klotter,. *A New History of Kentucky*. Lexington: The University Press of Kentucky, 1997.

Hopkins, Kate. *99 Drams of Whiskey: The Accidental Hedonist's Quest for the Perfect Shot and the History of the Drink*. New York: St. Martin's Press, 2009.

Kleber, John E., editor in chief, Thomas D. Clark, Lowell H. Harrison, and James C. Klotter, associate editors. *The Kentucky Encyclopedia*. Lexington: The University Press of Kentucky, 1992.

Linklater, Andro. *An Artist in Treason: The Extraordinary Double Life of General James Wilkinson*. New York: Walker Publishing Company, 2009.

Maurer, David W. *Kentucky Moonshine*. Lexington: The University Press of Kentucky, 1974.

McCullough, David. *The Pioneers: The Heroic Story of the Settlers Who Brought the American Ideal West*. New York: Simon & Schuster, 2019.

Minnick, Fred. *Bourbon: The Rise, Fall, and Rebirth of an American Whiskey*. Minneapolis, MN: Quarto Publishing Group, 2016.

Okrent, Daniel. *Last Call: The Rise and Fall of Prohibition*. New York, London: Scribner, 2010.

Pacult, F. Paul. *American Still Life: The Jim Beam Story and the Making of the World's #1 Bourbon*. Hoboken, NJ: John Wiley & Sons, 2003.

Peck, Garrett. *The Prohibition Hangover: Alcohol in America from Demon Rum to Cult Cabernet*. New Brunswick, NJ & London: Rutgers University Press, 2009.

Raitz, Karl. *Making Bourbon: A Geographical History of Distilling in Nineteenth-Century Kentucky*. Lexington: The University Press of Kentucky, 2020.

Riegler, Susan. *Kentucky Bourbon Country: The Essential Travel Guide*. Lexington: The University Press of Kentucky, 2013.

Risen, Clay. *American Whiskey Bourbon & Rye: A Guide to the Nation's Favorite Spirit*. New York: Sterling Epicure, 2013, revised 2015.

Roosevelt, Theodore. *The Winning of the West: Volume 2, From the Alleghanies to the Mississippi 1777–1783*. New York: G. P. Putnam's Sons, 1894. Nebraska: First Bison Book, 1995

Rothbaum, Noah. *The Business of Spirits: How Savvy Marketers, Innovative Distillers, and Entrepreneurs Changed How We Drink*. New York: Kaplan Publishing, 2007.

Rothbaum, Noah. *The Art of American Whiskey: A Visual History of the Nation's Most Storied Spirits, Through 100 Iconic Labels*. New York: Crown Publishing Group, 2015.

Slaughter, Thomas P. *The Whiskey Rebellion: Frontier Epilogue to the American Revolution*. New York/Oxford, England: Oxford University Press, 1986.

Taylor, Richard. *The Great Crossing: A Historic Journey to Buffalo Trace Distillery.* Frankfort, KY: Buffalo Trace Distillery, 2002.

Thompson, Wright. *Pappyland: A Story of Family, Fine Bourbon, and the Things That Last.* New York: Penguin Press, 2020.

Tramazzo, John C. *Bourbon & Bullets: True Stories of Whiskey, War, and Military Service.* Nebraska: Potomac Books, University of Nebraska Press, 2018.

Veach, Michael. *Kentucky Bourbon Whiskey: An American Heritage.* Lexington: University Press of Kentucky, 2013.

Weinstein, Allen, and David Rubel,. *The Story of America: Freedom and Crisis from Settlement to Superpower.* London, New York: DK Publishing, 2002.

Wondrich, David. *Imbibe! From Absinthe Cocktail to Whiskey Smash, a Salute in Stories and Drinks to "Professor" Jerry Thomas, Pioneer of the American Bar.* New York: Perigee Book/Penguin Group, 2007, revised 2015.

About the Author

F. PAUL PACULT **has been** hailed as ". . . an all-knowing spirituous oracle, a J.D. Power of liquor" by *Imbibe* magazine and "America's foremost spirits authority" by forbes.com. He is the author of seven books, including *American Still Life* (2003), *A Double Scotch* (2005), and *The New Kindred Spirits* (2021), and a contributor to two other books, all on beverage alcohol. From 1991 to 2019, he was the editor and sole reviewer of the quarterly, advertising-free, subscription-only newsletter, *F. Paul Pacult's Spirit Journal*. Since 1989, his writings have been published in the *New York Times* magazine, *Wine Enthusiast*, Delta Air Lines *SKY* in-flight magazine, *Playboy* magazine, *Cheers*, *Beverage Dynamics*, *MarketWatch*, *Mens Journal*, and scores of other publications.

Pacult has been honored multiple times in Scotland, France, and the United States for his contributions to beverage alcohol journalism, criticism, and education, including being named a life member of the *Bourbon Hall of Fame* in 2003 and the Kentucky Distillers Association's *Order of the Writ* in 2018. He has been a consultant to large and small beverage companies both on the creation of new spirits brands and the refreshing of established brands. As an educator, he is a cofounder of the award-winning company Beverage Alcohol Resource, and along with Sue Woodley created the celebrated trade education "Authority" series. In 2010, along with David Talbot and Sue Woodley, he established the beverage competition company, *Ultimate Beverage Challenge*, where he is Judging Director. Pacult also serves as Master Blender for the American whiskey brand Jacob's Pardon.

Pacult resides in New York's Hudson Valley with his wife and partner, Sue Woodley.

Index

Page references followed by *p* indicate a photograph.